OPTIONS TRADING

7 BOOK IN 1

The Complete Crash Course for Beginners to Learn How to Trade Like a Pro Using The Best Strategies to Maximize Your Profit | Reduce Risk of Loss As a Top 1% Trader.

NOAH SMITH

TABLE OF CONTENTS

BOOK 3

OPTION TRADING BASIC STRATEGIES

BOOK 4

OPTIONS TRADING TECHNICAL & FUNDAMENTAL ANALYSIS

BOOK 5

OPTIONS TRADING ADVANCED STRATEGIES

BOOK 6

PSYCHOLOGY OF TRADER

BOOK 7

OPTION TRADING GLOSSARY & FAQ

INTRODUCTION

Options are contracts that give the bearer the right but not the obligation to purchase or sell a certain amount of an underlying investment at a predetermined price on or before the expiration date of the contract. However, the bearer is not required to exercise this right or obligation. Options, much like the vast majority of other asset categories, can be obtained through the use of brokerage accounts.

The expiration date, also known as the day on which the option loses its validity and value,is a crucial element of all options, regardless of type. During the month until the expiry date, investors may sell their options to someone else for a profit. However, it will lose value as the option approaches its expiry date due to time decay and other factors.

The earliest options were used to wager on the olive crop in ancient Greece; nevertheless, current option contracts often relate to stocks. So, what exactly is a stock option, and where did it come from? A stock option contract allows the participant to acquire a predetermined percentage of investors at a set rate for a particular timeframe. Bucket shoppers, as they were nicknamed, began to appear as options.

Jesse Livermore, a guy from America in the 1920s, made the bucket store famous. Livermore was a stock market speculator who did not own the stocks he was speculating on and anticipated their future pricing. He started his business as a stock option bookie, taking the opposing side of anybody who anticipated the price of a certain stock would rise or fall. He would take the opposite side of the deal if someone told him that the stock of XYZ Company would go upward.

The commodities futures and stock options markets were plagued by extensive unlawful activity at the outset. The Chicago Board of Options Exchange is the most extensively traded option Exchange (CBOE). Like stock market activities, Options market operations are closely scrutinized by regulatory organizations such as the SEC and the FBI in certain circumstances. The commodities market is likewise heavily controlled nowadays. Through the Commodity Futures Trading Commission, the Commodity Exchange Act outlaws illicit futures trading and requires the industry's unique processes. Regulatory bodies are worried about several concerns, many of which derive from today's trading environment's high level of computerization. To provide equal playing space for all investors, the agencies strive to outlaw price manipulation and collusion.

The futures and options markets have been in existence for many decades. It's possible that some investors will be taken aback by this news given that they believed only Wall Street power players had access to stock futures and options. Futures markets were initially established by Japanese samurai in order to dominate the market on rice, whereas options may have their roots in the olive trade conducted in ancient Greece. In spite of the fact that these instruments were developed in a society that predates our own by several hundred years, they are still widely used today, which is evidence of the usefulness of these tools.

Option buyers have the ability, but not the obligation, to buy or sell the underlying stock at a predetermined price (known as the "strike price") on or before a predetermined date, provided that the strike price is reached. The transaction has to be completed by the vendor, which means that they are obligated to either buy or sell the underlying stock if the option's owner exercises it before the option's expiration date, whichever occurs first. In compensation for this privilege, the buyer pays him a premium. He benefits financially from this arrangement.

One of the most successful trading techniques that can be utilized in today's market is the utilization of options. They make it possible for traders to increase their profits on their existing portfolios, regulate the risk associated with their investments, and leverage their existing positions, among other benefits. Those who are interested in becoming successful options traders can achieve their goals with the help of the information provided in this book, which ranges from fundamental ideas to complicated trading techniques.

You have the option, when trading options, of playing the role of a two-dollar investor who bets on the movement of stocks, markets, futures, and commodities; alternatively, you can play the role of a casino or a regulated bookie who accepts bets rather than putting them themselves. You decide on the role and then enjoy and profit from it. It is not uncommon to make profits over 1000% when trading options, and it is possible to develop techniques that will win up to 90% of the time.

Better still, options are an amazing investing strategy that allows you to have much more flexibility while also reducing your risks and increasing your income in the financial markets, as shown here. Once you have learned how to correctly utilize options, you will be able to include this instrument in your financial portfolio for the rest of your life.

Options provide investors with a plethora of different techniques to consider. Certain options are very cautious, such as covered call writing, while others are extremely speculative, such as naked call selling. When it comes to fine-tuning your investment methods to anticipated market circumstances, options provide more and often better options than ever before.

Both bullish and negative tactics are discussed in equal measure. Everyone who trades options or hedges their portfolios can benefit from this book, from beginners to experts.

This book will discuss everything about options trading from beginner to advanced level.

You will discover that you can trade more than just stocks once you begin trading. You can, in fact, trade money, options, and commodities. Some trades will be more dangerous than others. The type of trading you do will frequently be determined by the level of risk you are willing to accept.

A trading career allows traders to live the life they want by providing them with Financial Freedom that takes money out of the equation, Flexibility to work from anywhere in the world, and Independence to answer only to themselves while having no boss or superior to control their life.

Many people aspire to this lifestyle, but only a few are successful. People fail not because they are not smart or lucky enough, but because they lack basic knowledge and fail to find proper guidance (rules) to become a successful trader.

This book will teach dedicated readers the fundamentals of trading, which they can put into practice.

Many factors must be considered to trade successfully, one of which is changing one's mindset. One should be aware of how they have been programmed to think, and with the information available about trading and the stock market, one can easily change their thinking to capitalize on a profitable trading opportunity.

Another aspect that traders must embrace to trade successfully is planning. Many traders believe that more trading equals more profits, which is not always the case with day trading. A plan will help you focus on quality trades rather than quantity trades, with the former being more advantageous.

Above all, learn everything you can. There is a lot of information available that you can use.

Knowledge is power, and it will always help you trade successfully.
So, let's start!

BOOK 1

OPTIONS TRADING FOR BEGINNERS

CHAPTER 1

How to Make Money with Options?

The majority of options traders utilize options to leverage their market-timing selections. They purchase call options when they believe an advance is near, and they purchase put options when they believe a drop is impending. Unfortunately, since purchasing calls and puts entails purchasing a waste asset, this technique is often unproductive in the long run. Most individuals who trade options, it is believed, lose money in the long term (90% or more of them). If this is accurate, it is an astonishing amount of money. While the high failure rate is shocking, it is not unexpected given the intricacy required in options trading. Most options traders do not take the time to build a well-thought-out trading strategy before trading in the market. In addition, many traders are ill-prepared to cope with the emotional side of trading, which is a common occurrence.

1.1 Probability in Option Trading

Options trading is essentially a game of chance. To be successful at trading options, people who want to do so must concentrate on continually putting the odds in their favor on a trade-by-trade basis rather than on the overall market. Another important component in determining if a possible trade or collection of deals will result in a profit or a loss is determining

the likelihood of profit or loss. The expectations for the majority of options transactions, on the other hand, are not as simple.

For this reason, and since option pricing contains a time premium that will be gone by the time of expiry, an option buyer nearly always has a lower than 50% chance of profiting. Still, an option writer almost always has a higher than 50% chance of profiting. In exchange, although purchasers of naked options benefit from the promise of infinite profit potential and little risk, they also benefit from a lesser likelihood of profiting from their investments. On the other hand, writers of naked options benefit from a greater chance of profit while also accepting a limited profit potential and an infinite risk.

1.2 Option Profitability

Those who buy call options put themselves in a position to profit if the price of an underlying asset (such as a stock, for example) rises above the "strike price" designated in the call contract at any point prior to the expiration date of the call contract. This can occur at any time before the expiration date of the call contract. The owner of a put option, on the other hand, stands to make a profit if the value of the underlying commodity drops just below the strike price (also known as the reference price) well in advance of the option's expiration date. This is because the strike price and the reference price are synonymous terms. A call option writer (seller) has the intention of making a profit from the transaction in the event that the underlying stock market evaluation remains lower than the strike price for the duration of the contract period. This is because the call option writer expects the underlying stock market evaluation to remain lower than the strike price. When an investor purchases a put option, they are positioning themselves to make a profit if the price of the underlying commodity remains at or above the target price of the option contract. In this kind of arrangement, the only source of revenue that the option writer has access to is the payment that is charged for the call-and-put contract.

1.3 Calculating Probability

Position	Momentum	ADX Value > 25	ADX Value < 25
DI+ above DI-	Indicates Uptrend	Strong Uptrend	Weak, Unsustainable Uptrend
DI- above DI+	Indicates Downtrend	Strong Downtrend	Weak, Unsustainable Downtrend

What Does POP (PROBABILITY OF PROFIT) Stand For?

When it comes to selling options, the likelihood of making a profit is determined by a number of different variables, including the following: Our options are sold at strike values that are either "in the money," which indicates that the underlying stock price is currently trading, "at the money," which indicates that the stock price is currently not trading, or "out of the money," which indicates that the price of the underlying stock is currently not trading (at a better price than where the stock price is trading). When everything is taken into account, we might reach the conclusion that if we think that buying or selling all of the shares will result in a chance to flip a coin, we will have a success rate that is greater than fifty percent of the time.

This could be the case if we believe that the toss of the coin will determine whether we buy or sell all of the shares. Our chances of being successful significantly increase whenever we make use of strategies such as these. Even if the stock price stays the same, moves slightly in our favour, or moves slightly in the opposing direction, once the option's term has run its course and expired, we will still be profitable.

Selling Profit Probability

Your chances of being successful in life as a whole are improved when you have a number of different career paths open to you from which you can generate income. When we sell options, we generate a credit, which can be conceptualized in the same way that one might think of money operating in the economy. It is possible for us to make use of this credit to protect ourselves from potential losses in our circumstances; as a result, the likelihood of our being successful will be increased as a direct result of this action. Since our POP is directly related to our breakeven price, which rises when we sell premium, we have the potential to continuously raise our product's perceived value (POP) with strategies that involve selling premium. This is because our breakeven price rises when we sell premium.

Buying Profit Probability

When purchasing options, the likelihood of earning a profit can be broken down as follows: the term "buying spreads" is more commonly used when referring to the act of "purchasing options." Because we have no means of hedging the cost of the option, purchasing a naked option is the riskiest thing we can do for our breakeven. As a result, it is the worst thing we can do for our breakeven. As a result of this, we are absolutely committed to disseminating. When we buy spreads, the breakeven price of a spread needs to be close to or slightly better than the present stock price in order for us to make a profit. It guarantees that the Percentage will be close to fifty percent, or a little bit higher than that.

Probability of Profit on Cost Reduction

The inclusion of a free short option in the transaction is among the advantages of stock ownership that provide the greatest value. That places money—not profit—in our wallets right away and eliminates the need to acquire any additional buying power. We might be able to decrease the cost basis of our stock while simultaneously acquiring a bonus if we issue one call option for every one hundred shares of stock that we own, and we might be able to use the premium to do so. It switches the odds of winning in investments from a coin flip of 50/50 to a much greater probability of being successful. It is now possible for the stock to remain precisely where it is, move slightly in either direction, and for us to still make a profit depending on the credit that we get when we sell the call option. Because we can never be sure of the direction in which stocks will move, we concentrate our efforts on increasing the only aspect of our investment that is under our direct control: the cost foundation.

1.4 Evaluating Risk Tolerance

To maximize your profits, specify if you would be better suited as an option buyer or an option writer. Consider the following scenario: you have the opportunity to purchase or write 10 call option contracts at $0.50 per call. In most cases, each contract includes 100 shares as the underlying asset. Thus, a total of 10 contracts would cost $500 ($0.50 times 100 times 10 contracts). In the example above, if you purchase 10 call option contracts for $500, you may sustain the potential amount will be $500. Your potential profit, on the other hand, is potentially endless. So, what exactly is the catch? The likelihood that the deal will be lucrative is not particularly great. However, if you write 10 call option contracts, your total revenue is restricted to the premium revenue received, which is $500. Your maximum loss is, on the other hand, potentially limitless. At 75%, the likelihood of a good options deal is quite high in your favor, indicating that you should proceed with caution. So, would you be willing to risk $500, recognizing that you should have a 75% probability of losing your money and a 25% chance of generating a return on your investment? Alternatively, would you like to earn a maximum of $500, realizing that you will have a 75% probability of retaining the whole amount or a portion of it, but a 25% risk of losing the entire balance or a portion of it in the trade?

The answers to these questions will provide you with an indication of your risk appetite and whether you might be better off as an option buyer or option writer in the future. It is crucial to remember that generalized numbers apply to all options. At some periods, it may be more advantageous to be an option writer or a buyer in a certain asset rather than the other way around. The use of the appropriate method at an adequate moment can drastically modify these probabilities.

CHAPTER 2

Why Invest in Options Trading?

2.1 How New Technology Has Changed Investing

The widespread use of smartphones and enhanced Internet access has altered how people interact with technology today and has led to the collapse or extinction of conventional enterprises in certain cases. Despite the fact that modern stock traders have access to an infinite amount of data and highly sophisticated trading instruments, many investors fail to recognize the humble beginnings of investing as well as the various technological advancements that have significantly altered financial markets. From the very first stock to the complex trading algorithms used today, the advancement of investing technology has always been driven by the pursuit of a singular objective: the most effective use of capital to generate profits for companies and their shareholders.

Companies operating in fields as disparate as journalism, finance, and transportation services have been forced in recent years to reevaluate the marketing approaches they are currently utilizing for their businesses.

Traditional media businesses have been forced to reconsider the ways in which they engage with their audience as a result of the proliferation of online and mobile streaming services, such as Netflix, as well as a host of other similar services.

The financial technology sector, also known as fintech, is one more that exemplifies why traditional businesses need to adapt to new technologies in order to compete effectively with newer, more innovative competitors. For many years, banks have maintained an iron grip on the manner in which individuals carry out their financial transactions.

On the other hand, disruptors are presenting new ways to earn money and receive it through the use of the internet. Companies such as TransferWise and Toast allow money to be sent over the internet and collected in person, and Alipay and WeChat Pay have revolutionized the way people pay for goods and services. Today, companies such as TransferWise and Toast allow money to be sent over the internet and collected in person. Technology and finance are two fields that are always progressing in their respective fields. Each industry is becoming more reliant on the others. Failure to keep up with contemporary technologies and master new skills might cause you to fall behind and suffer a financial setback.

2.2 Why Should You Invest in Options Trading?

Options have been accessible for close to four decades, but we are just now starting to give them the attention they warrant. Many potential investors have avoided options due to the widespread perception that these financial instruments are overly complicated and difficult to grasp. Because neither they nor their advisors received sufficient training on how to use options effectively, a much larger number of people have had negative experiences with them. The improper application of options, much like the mishandling of any powerful technology, can result in serious problems. Finally, the financial media and well-known market personalities have mistakenly associated "risky" or "hazardous" options. On the other hand, individual investors should obtain all sides of the story before deciding on the value of options.

Options may provide an investor with four significant benefits (in no particular order):

- They may result in greater cost-effectiveness.

- They could be less hazardous than stocks.

- They have a larger chance of delivering bigger returns of percentage.

- They provide a variety of expertise options.

Efficiency in Terms of Cost

Options provide a significant amount of flexibility. As a consequence of this, an investor might have an option position that is the same as a stock position but at a significantly reduced cost. For instance, an investor must spend $16,000 in order to purchase 200 shares of a company that costs $80 each. On the other hand, if the investor decided to purchase two $20 calls, each of which would represent 100 shares, the total expenditure would be reduced to just $4,000. This would be the result of two contracts being multiplied by 100 shares per contract and the current market price of $20. After that, the investor would have an additional $12,000 available to spend however they saw appropriate.

Things aren't quite as simple as they seem at first glance. It is necessary for the investor to select the most appropriate call option to acquire in order to accurately replicate the stock position. On the other hand, this strategy for stock replenishment is doable, sensible, and efficient in its use of resources.

Example: Let's say you've decided to invest in the stock of XYZ Corporation on the assumption that it will appreciate in value over the course of the next few months. You have decided that you want to buy 200 shares of XYZ at a price of $131 per share, which will cost you a total of $26,200. You could have gone to the options exchange, choose an option that roughly matched the stock, and paid $34 for an August call option that had a strike price of $100. This would have given you the opportunity to buy the stock at a price of $100. This would have prevented you from having to risk such a large amount of money. You would need to buy two contracts if you wanted to have an interest equal to the value of the previously mentioned 200 shares. The difference might be saved in your account and compounded over time, or it could be invested in another opportunity with more diversification potential, for example.

Lower Risk (If Used Properly)

There are situations in which purchasing options present a higher level of risk than purchasing shares, but there are also scenarios in which options can be used to reduce risk exposure. It is entirely dependent on the purpose you have in mind for using them. Investors may view options as less risky than stocks due to the fact that options require less of a financial investment on their part, and investors may also view options as less risky due to the fact that options are relatively impervious to the potentially catastrophic impacts of gap openings.

Options provide the most consistent method of balancing, which places them in a more advantageous position than stocks. When an individual purchases stocks, they will frequently place a stop-loss order in order to protect their investment from potential losses. The stop order protects the purchaser from incurring losses that are greater than or equal to a predetermined price. The problem with these instructions is that they are of the same kind as other similar instructions. When the stock price drops to the limit that was mentioned in the stop order or lower, the stop order is carried out.

Example: Imagine for a moment that you have acquired ABC, Inc. shares worth $50 in total. Because you don't want to lose more than 10% of your investment, you place a stop order for $45 to protect yourself from further losses. This order to sell will be converted into a market order to sell the asset as soon as it trades at or below 45 dollars. This procedure works well during the day, but it could present some difficulties later in the evening. Suppose you decide to go to bed with the range at $51. The following morning, when you wake up and turn on CNBC, you find out that there has been breaking news regarding your company. Since quite some time ago, it would appear that the CEO of the business has been lying about the company's profit reports, and there are even allegations that he has embezzled money. It is anticipated that the share price will open the trading session with a loss of approximately $20. In the event that this takes place, the price of the first transaction that falls below your stop order's maximum price of $45 will be $20. Therefore, in order to lock in a substantial loss, you decide to sell the stock at its opening price of $20. You were unable to use the stop-loss order precisely when you required it the most.

If you had purchased a put option as a form of protection, you could have avoided the catastrophic loss that you went through. Futures, in contrast to stop-loss orders, continue to be valid after the market has closed for the day. They provide you with protection against your insurance risks twenty-four hours a day, seven days a week. Stop orders are ineffectual tools for accomplishing this objective. As a result of this, trading with options is generally regarded as a reliable method of risk management.

In addition, you could have used the stock substitution technique that was discussed earlier in this paragraph to buy an in-the-money call instead of the stock in order to replace the stock in your portfolio. This would have accomplished the same goal as purchasing the stock. There are some options that can replicate up to 85 percent of the performance of a business while only costing a portion of the price of the stock. These options are known as "replicators." If you had bought the call option with a strike price of $45 rather than the shares, the maximum amount of money that you could have lost is equivalent to the amount that you paid for the option.

If you had paid $6 for the option, rather than the $31 you would have lost if you had purchased the stock, you would have only lost $6 because you would have paid for the option. When compared to the natural and full-time stop that is supplied by options, stop orders are ineffective.

Increased Potential Profits

You won't need to do any calculations to figure out that your percentage return will be higher if you spend less money but generate profits that are roughly the same as before. When an option pays off, most of them grant the investor something along those lines.

Example: In the scenario that was presented earlier, we are going to look at the percentage returns of both the stock (which was purchased for $50) and the option (which was obtained for $6). Let's say the option has a delta of 80; this indicates that the price of the option will fluctuate by 80% of the price movement in the company. Let's look at an example. If the price of the stock was increased to $5, the profit on your investment would be 10%. Your options position would earn $4, which is equal to 80% of the stock's movement, because it has a delta of 80. When compared to the stock's 10% return, a gain of $4 on an expenditure of $6 results in a return of 67%. This is a significant improvement. Naturally, if the business transaction does not go in your favor, the available choices may be expensive: there is a possibility that you will lose all of your money.

Additional Strategic Options

The provision of additional opportunities for financial investment brings us to the fourth essential advantage of choices. Choices are a very useful instrument that can be put to work in a number of different ways. It is possible to recreate many different scenarios by selecting from a number of different options. These kinds of situations are known as synthetic positions.

Investors have access to a multitude of choices, which may work to their advantage when striving to accomplish the same financial goals when using synthetic positions. Choices provide a wide range of strategic possibilities, despite the fact that synthetic circumstances are more difficult to understand. When wanting to short a company, for instance, a lot of investors turn to brokers who make them pay a margin. It's possible that the price of satisfying this margin requirement will be quite expensive. Some investors choose to work with companies that do not permit shorting of stocks under any circumstances. Because investors are unable to play the downside when it is necessary, they are forced to exist in a world of black-and-white while the market trades in color. This effectively hands investors the ability to be handcuffed. One significant benefit of options dealing is that investors are not restricted by their broker from purchasing puts in order to "play the downside."

Investors also have the ability to trade the market's "third dimension," also known as "no direction," through the use of options trading. Investors are able to trade market movements as well as time and volatility fluctuations through the use of options. The vast majority of the time, the majority of stocks do not go through significant price fluctuations. Very few companies experience large price swings, and even those that do so infrequently. Your capacity to profit from stagnation may prove to be the deciding factor in whether or not your monetary goals will be realized, or whether they will continue to be a pipe fantasy. The only way to obtain the necessary strategic options to be successful in any industry is to have choices.

2.3 Options Trading Reduces Your Risks

Numerous investors find that options are an excellent instrument for risk management. They perform the function of a hedge against falls in asset prices. If an investor is concerned that the price of the LMN Corporation shares he owns will decrease, he or she may decide to purchase puts. Purchasing puts grants the investor the right to sell the stock at the strike price, regardless of how much lower the market price falls before the option expires. By spending the option premium, the investor has protected themselves against losses that occur at prices that are lower than the strike price. This type of option strategy also goes by the name "hedging using a protective put," which is yet another name for the strategy. Bear in mind that even though trading with options might help you reduce risk, investments in general carry some level of uncertainty. When it comes to returns, there is no assurance whatsoever. Individuals who use options as a risk management tool are always looking for new ways to cut the amount of money they could potentially lose. They might decide to purchase options because the maximum amount of money they stand to lose is equal to the premium they pay. In compensation, they are granted the right to buy or sell the underlying securities at a fair price during the term of the option. They stand to gain financially from an increase in the value of the option's premium in the event that they decide against exercising the option and instead offer it back to the market. Because option writers are sometimes required to buy or sell shares at an unfavorable price, the risk associated with certain short positions may be heightened.

Several different methods for using options seek to reduce risk by hedging already existing portfolios. Although alternatives can act as safety blankets, one should be aware that they do not come risk-free. As a result of the rapid opening and closing of transactions, it is possible to make rapid progress toward one's goals. It's possible for losses to mount up at the same pace as gains. It is essential that you have a solid understanding of the dangers associated with buying, selling, and holding options before you decide to include them in your investment portfolio.

2.4 Why Is Options Trading Becoming More Popular?

Although selling options has been around for quite some time, it is only recently becoming available to the general public, and there has been a significant surge in the number of people engaging in this activity.

Before the advancements made in the preceding decade, almost all options trading was conducted by institutional investors, major businesses, and individuals with high net worth. This was due to the fact that opening a trading account with a reputable bank required a significant amount of capital. Displays used to be cluttered with cell after cell of flashing data, making it difficult for users to make sense of patterns and making it necessary for dealers to figure out patterns on their own. Today, however, the standard options trading experience is much more user-friendly. Because it was necessary to plan a path through these screens and have precise predictions for how the market would move, options trading was almost always delegated to specialized professionals.

On the other hand, options trading has undergone significant change over the past few years as a direct result of the emergence of fintech companies that have entered the market in order to capitalize on the rapid development of technology. These organizations have made the practise of selling options accessible to a new and larger market; as a result, anyone with an investment capital of as little as one thousand dollars can now begin incorporating options into their strategies.

Additionally, fintech companies have developed new and improved desktop platforms that are easy to comprehend and use, as well as new smartphone platforms, which have simplified the process of opening new accounts, gaining access to existing accounts, and managing existing accounts. Many of the headaches that are normally associated with traditional options trading have been alleviated as a result of the development of dedicated features that provide all of the necessary information to support trade, automatically perform any necessary calculations to lay out the stakes, and provide vivid and easily understandable visualizations of how a trade might play out, including potential profits and losses. These interactive interfaces even go as far as to provide comprehensive descriptions of various techniques, along with the scenarios in which they are effective, as well as simplified methods for putting each technique into practise.

Trading options now look very different than it did in the past thanks to the proliferation of online trading platforms, which have made the actual dealing and the understanding of the risks involved much less difficult. Traders of every stripe are now in a situation where they can maximize their profits by putting into action a method or a strategy that corresponds to the way they see the market and maximizes their profits.

CHAPTER 3
Options Trading Basics

The provision and sale of specified stock trading volumes at a defined price throughout a specified trading term before the expiry date is the primary function of an options contract.

3.1 What Are Options

When an option is purchased or sold, it grants the buyer or vendor the right to buy or sell a commodity, payment fund, or index for a limited time at a predetermined price. To be explicit, investors are not obligated to purchase or sell any particular item at any particular price. The options market is a marketplace where interested parties buy and sell contracts. By purchasing a call option, investors gain the right to purchase additional shares at a later date, whereas those who purchase put options gain the right to sell preferred stock at a later date.

Options are not the same as stock option grants because options do not indicate company ownership. Options are a lower-risk investment compared to futures due to the ability to withdraw from an options contract at any point during the trading session. Option premiums are typically expressed as a fraction of the value of the underlying stock or other assets.

The buyer or seller of an option retains the right to exercise the option at any time prior to its expiration date; therefore, facilitating the transfer or sale of an option does not necessarily imply that the option must be exercised immediately following the purchase or sale, or at any time in the future. Options are considered derivative securities because their values are derived from those of other assets. Many people believe options to be a more secure investment than stocks for this and other reasons.

Why would a financial supporter want to use options in the first place? Contracts to purchase stocks are wagers on the price's future rise or decline.

By engaging into an options contract, you can determine the "premium," or the cost of purchasing an option contract, and the "strike price," or the agreed-upon price at which you'll purchase the underlying financial instrument. When selecting a strike price, you are essentially wagering on whether the underlying asset's value will rise. The premium on a wager is a fixed percentage of the asset's value.

Call options give the investor the right (but not the obligation) to sell their stocks at a specified future date, while put options give the investor the right (but not the obligation) to buy their stocks at that future date.

3.2 Types of Options

Following are the types of options trading.

- call option
- Put options

Call Options

The investor in a call contract has the legal right, for the duration of the contract, to buy 100 shares of the underlying asset or commodity at a set price per share. To illustrate, a call option gives an investor the right to buy shares of a particular stock, bond, or other financial product (like an exchange-traded fund or index) at a predetermined price and time (by the expiration of the contract).

A call option buyer is betting on an increase in the stock's (or asset's) price so they can cash in by exercising their option to acquire shares at a higher price (and then usually immediately sell them to cash in on the profit).

Call premium is the expense of acquiring a call option (it is simply the cost of purchasing the contract that will allow you to purchase the stock or investment). The price paid for a call option can be thought of in the same way as a down payment on a house or car. Buying a call option gives you the right, at a predetermined price, to buy the underlying assets from the seller (until the contract expires).

To that end, call options are not dissimilar to reinsurance in that both enable you to buy an asset (in this case, stock) at a predetermined price for a limited time (which will not increase even if the price of the stock rises) But, your choice has to be refreshed (usually weekly, monthly or quarterly basis). Because of this, options will always be susceptible to time decay, which means that their value will gradually diminish over time.

Call options have a higher worth because of their inherent scarcity when the strike price is lower.

Put Options

When options traders enter into a put contract, they are committing to the legal obligation but not the duty to sell short (offer to sell) a certain number of shares of the underlying asset at a specified price within a specified time frame. Put options can be bought or sold on leverage through the stock market. The strike price of a put option is the price at which the option holder can transfer the underlying asset to the option grantor.

The fundamental assets on which put options are traded include stocks, currencies, bonds, commodities, futures, and indices, among many others. In opposition to a call option, which gives its holder the right to buy the underlying securities at a predetermined price on or before the option contract's expiration date, a put option gives its holder the right to sell those securities before the option contract's expiration date.

The worth of a put option rises when the underlying bond stock or investment's volatility declines. Instead, a put option loses value as stock prices increase. Due to this, they are frequently used for a balancing purpose.

A defensive put is a type of financial strategy. Put options are a common form of investment insurance or hedging used to ensure a stock's value declines by no more than a predetermined amount. To protect themselves from falling stock prices, investors can buy call options on the stocks they already own. If the trader is given the choice, he or she can sell the stock at the strike price. If the investor didn't already own shares of the underlying company prior to the execution of the put option, this is the position that will be formed.

3.3 Options Trading Tips for Beginners

The following easy options trading recommendations for beginners will help you get started in the universe of options trading or will help you determine whether trading options are a suitable match for your overall investing plan.

Think Flexibly

Unlike conventional investing, where you strive to buy cheap and sell high, options trading requires you to think flexibly. Traders may make money by forecasting downswings, immobility, and widespread volatility, along with upturns, in the market using options. Because of the variable nature of options trading, traders who are new to the market have a great deal more to consider when deciding on a course of action. Prepare yourself to seek out and exploit possibilities in unfamiliar environments. With more trading freedom come new ways of achieving success, and new strategies, in turn, lead to new approaches. The "straddling" strategy, for example, enables options traders to benefit by correctly forecasting the volatility of a stock's price.

This strategy will yield profits for the trader regardless of how much the stock rises or falls in value. This form of flexible position is predominant in options trading, but it is uncommon in other types of investments, such as mutual funds.

Use Option to Hedge

Options trading can be used to hedge risks. Options trading allows investors to reduce their risk exposure. If you are predictable about the reliability of security but do not decide to sell it, options provide a way to protect your investment. A common strategy is to purchase a put option on the stock, which will authorize you to get around at a reasonable price unless the stock dives into the short term. Such hedging potential is primarily abundant in the options trading market, and they serve as a compelling argument for investors to consider dipping their toes into the options trading waters. There is a curriculum, but no guarantees in life. Even the most seasoned options traders recognize there is no such thought as a risk-free investment strategy entirely.

Purchase and Sell Stocks at a Price That You Determine

Smart options traders utilize options to fine-tune their overall investing approach rather than relying on them entirely. In other words, they should make the most out of their tireless market information. When you buy options, you are purchasing the opportunity to purchase a commodity at a specific price and time in the future. While most simple investing platforms will enable you to establish preferred buying and selling values for stocks, the purchase, sale, and exercise of options may significantly increase your earning potential by considerably increasing your profit margins. In the stock market, strategies also including covered calls and revenue puts may provide individuals more discretion and revenue potential when purchasing and selling stocks. Take the time to look at and analyze some of the most effective options trading approaches and strategies available.

Know Your Break-Even Points

There is a break-even point for every option you purchase or sell. Knowing your break-even marks will help you avoid making one of the most common errors when investing with options failing to comply with your trading plan, and losing money.

To begin turning a fortune from an option, the stock price must rise or fall to a certain point (either high or low) before the option owner may begin making a profit.

When calculating break-even marks, it is necessary to compensate for both the amount paid to acquire the option and any fees payable on the buy and sell trades.

Have an Escape Plan

Check your impulses at the door when trading options, just like you would when trading stocks. Already have exit strategies in mind when trading options. Although no one is a robot, trading is a legitimate business. Make a strategy, keep to the plan, then put the plan into action. In sequence to do so, you must have a well-stated departure plan. Exit tactics are beneficial in various situations, not simply when things are going badly. It is also vital to recognize when it is time to go, even when everything is going your way.

Or, to put it another way, don't hold on to trades that are going downhill because you are emotionally committed to them. Please don't get carried away with investments that have already achieved their price goals out of greed. Would you instead take a chance on a one-time accomplishment or preserve your psychological stress moderate while earning a consistent income? Don't stray from the course of action. Even if making the appropriate decisions whenever trading options is critical, understanding the pitfalls that should be avoided is even more critical. Although winning is always the aim, there are times when the most anyone can do is avoid losing.

3.4 Expiration Time and Liquidity

Expiration Time

The precise day and time when an options contract or other commodity is deemed null and invalid is the expiry time. Financial derivatives contracts that are out of the money (OTM) will be deemed worthless when they mature. Still, contracts that are in the money (ITM) will be valued based on the settlement market value at the time of termination will be considered valuable. Although the expiry time is more exact than the expiration date, the two terms should not be misconstrued with the final moment an option might be traded.

It is essential to distinguish between the expiry time and the expiration date. The expiry date is the final day on which the option owner may exercise their option, which means that the exercise notice must have been received by that date to be effective. It indicates that the desires of the option holder should always be known sometime before the expiry time.

Note that during investing via a broker, the expiry periods and dates may differ from when investing directly. The timeframes may be anything from half an hour to as many hours early as possible to provide the broker with enough time to complete their client's order. The difference between the two is defined by the broker and the regulations that they have put down in advance. In the end, it gives the broker enough time to notify the exchange of the option holders' intentions before the option's expiration date arrives. Aside from that, contingent on which marketplace the option is being transacted on, the timeframes might differ as well.

The majority of options contracts ultimately complete their expiry date because traders close their holdings before the contract's expiration date arrives. Options that remain active until their expiry date have a more significant number of variables to consider than options that do not.

Liquidity

One measure of a stock or option's liquidity is how easily it can be bought and sold without having a significant effect on its present market price. Despite the fact that tradable options can be bought and sold more quickly and at a lower price than illiquid options, the availability of tradable options is still a major factor in the options dealing market. This means that it could take more time to join or exit a trade at a price close to its present value, and that your transaction could have an effect on the price of the asset, resulting in a lower entry or exit price.

3.5 Risk and Benefits in Options Trading

Options provide investors with more analytical (and economic) flexibility than they can get around merely purchasing, selling, or shorting equities. Market circumstances vary, and traders may use options to protect their portfolios from losses, buy a stock for far less than trades on the marketplace (or sell it for more), improve the yield on current or future holdings, and reduce the risk on speculative wagers in a variety of situations.

Benefits (Advantages) of Options Trading

The Initial Financial Investment Is Smaller Than That Required for Stock Trading

The cost of purchasing an option (which includes the premium and trading charge) is far less than the cost of purchasing shares directly, which would be much more. The options shareholders receive minimal out-of-pocket money to participate in the same game, but if the deal goes their way, they will earn just as much (in terms of percentage gains) as the investor who paid a lot of money for the stock in the first place.

Limited Downside of Options Buyers

As the buyer of an option, you are under no obligation to complete the transaction upon receiving a put or call. Let's say you were wrong about the time and direction of a stock's trajectory in your estimates. In that case, your liabilities are limited to the amount you charged for the agreement and any trading costs you incurred during that period. On the other hand, the negative might be far more prominent for option sellers—read the disadvantages section below for more information.

Flexibility for Traders

Options provide traders with built-in flexibility in the following ways:

- There are various strategic movements that investors may make before an options contract expires, including the following:
  o They should exercise their option and purchase the shares to increase the size of their portfolio.

If you sell your option contract to someone else before it expires, you may be capable of recovering the money you spent on an "out of the money" option purchase.

Options Allow an Investor to Set the Price of a Stock

Options contracts function similarly to a layaway plan in that they enable investors to "lay down" a certain amount of money (the strike price) in exchange for "locking in" the stock price at that level for a certain period of time (the expiration date). Depending on the type of option used and the timing of the execution, investors will have the ability to buy or sell shares of stock at a predetermined "striking price" at any time during the period.

Risks (Disadvantages) in Options Trading

Investing in options has a multitude of dangers, just like any other kind of investing. The following are some of the most significant dangers involved

Massive Damages

The option seller may suffer losses that exceed the amount of the contract's purchase price. Because the options are highly leveraged, their prices can fluctuate extremely fast. With options, you may see massive price swings in a brief period, such as minutes instead of just hours or days, as is the case with stock trading.

For those who are new to the game, it might be challenging. Many speculators are drawn to options trading because of its leverage, which allows them to make more money with less capital. Trading options is a sophisticated endeavor that needs a great deal of information and insight on the trader's part.

Short Term Investment

Options are short-term investments, and as a result, they may be held for a few days, weeks, or months. There is very little time left to recuperate the losses sustained. Consequently, the possibilities of losing a lot of money are proportional to the chances of winning significant gains from it in this situation.

Changes in Price

Because options are derivatives of stocks, even a slight fluctuation in the underlying stocks' or index's price may trigger a sudden and sharp change in the price of an option.

A person may reduce the risks he faces if he has a thorough and clear grasp of the company's strategy.

CHAPTER 4
Tips and Tricks for Success

1. Don't put more money into anything than you can afford to lose. Remember that options trading is a high-risk endeavor, and if your assumptions are incorrect or your timing is off, you might lose your whole investment. Start modestly, with options trading accounting for no more than 10% to 15% of your whole portfolio.

2. Conduct thorough research. Don't rush into an investment just because someone suggested it. Before you make a transaction, do your homework and make an educated conclusion.

3. Change your plan as market circumstances change. No one method will work in all markets. Keep up with what's going on in the economy and financial markets, and adjust your trading tactics to reflect market circumstances.

4. Before you buy, figure out how you'll get out. Create a strategy and stick to it. Allowing your emotions to override your sensible conclusions is not a good idea. Choose your upside and downside exit points, as well as your timeline, and don't get carried away with the prospect of more rewards.

5. Don't take on any more danger than you can handle. Determine your risk tolerance and develop techniques that remain inside that range. You don't want to be up at night worrying about whether or not you've made the appropriate investing choices.

6. Recognize when it's time to change your strategy. While having a strategy is critical in options trading, recognizing when your project needs improvement is also critical. Even though your emotions urge you to adhere to your plan, there will be occasions when you must deviate from it. When a trader's aim no longer applies to the present scenario, he or she is successful. Having a plan establishes your course, but it does not imply that you would mindlessly follow it until the end of the earth. Every trader reaches a time when something beyond their control occurs, rendering their strategy ineffective in that scenario. That is why, while making a strategy, be aware of its flaws and potential for failure. Market circumstances are always changing, so what is true now may not be true tomorrow. So, if you're thinking of sticking to your preset course of action even though market circumstances have shifted 180 degrees, you're making a huge error.

7. Before you begin, be sure you have a plan for your exit and entry. One of the most important skills to master is determining the best entry and exit points when it comes to options trading. No matter how brilliant your adjusting skills are, nothing can make up for a bad entrance. However, it would help if you broke away from this mindset. It might be a significant barrier for any novice trader. As long as you have a sound and lucrative trading strategy, you will earn from multiple deals in the future.

8. Trades that aren't in the money should be avoided. A few tactics may help you earn on out-of-the-money call options, but they are the exception. You could be drawn to out-of-the-money call options as a beginning investor in options trading since they are reasonable and cheap. It would also help if you kept in mind that

the stock market and the options market are two distinct circumstances.

9. Begin with enough funding. Although you do not need much cash to start, you should have enough to get your business up and running. In layman's words, wealth is the amount of money you should have in your trading account to cover any transaction costs, and this same capital will also protect you if you lose money while trading. You should always have some money in your trading account. When making trades, you should not be concerned about financial transfers, and the fact that the money is already in your account suggests that everything will go well.

10. Don't buy too much with your margin. The term margin was defined at the start of this book. It occurs when you borrow money from your broker to acquire options. In certain circumstances, margins may help you earn more money; but if you lose money, the losses will become much more accentuated due to the margins.

New workers are prone to get carried away because they believe margins equate to free money, so they continue to utilize them until the nightmare arrives. Assume you've employed margin, but the investment has now deteriorated.

BOOK 2

OPTIONS TRADING BASICS

CHAPTER 1

Options Trading

Because of their adaptability, options are a popular way to participate in the stock market. However, this implies that the investor should be aware of their risk appetite to avoid losing more money than they can afford.

Another reason it appeals to most investors is that it allows them to maintain control over their positions even if the market index fluctuates.

1.1 What Are the Options?

A simple definition of an Option is a legally binding agreement granting the holder the right, on a specified date and at a specified price, to buy or sell the underlying acquisition. This means that you have the ability to fix the value of stock purchases in advance, regardless of fluctuations in the market during the term of your contract. One contract for stock options typically represents one hundred shares of equity. The appeal of the options contract is that it binds the buyer and seller to a contract with certain characteristics and conditions to reduce the chance of losing money.

1.2 How Do Options Work?

Consider the case where you desire to acquire McDonald's shares (NYSE MCD) later. The stock is now trading at $101 per share. Based on their present condition, they are doing rather well, with stock prices expected to rise in the future time. So, you buy a call option

(Which is a sort of options contract that will be covered later in this book) and gain the right to buy McDonald's stocks at $101.

You have decided to acquire 10 stocks at $101 each in precisely 60 days. You are free to wait now that you have signed the contract. After 55 days, you see a rise in stock prices. It is now $200 per share. But, since you had an option contract to purchase 10 shares of McDonald's stock at $101 apiece, you were able to obtain it for a good price. That is the ideal situation.

Consider a situation in which the price drops. Consider how, instead of growing in price, McDonald's stock has dropped to $50 per share. In this situation, you would lose money on the options contract, and you would never buy stocks for $101 if the current price is $50 per share.

In this case, you will let the options contract expire and instead buy the stocks for $50 a share.

That's all there is to it. The truth is that you've been trading for a long time and aren't even aware of it. Consider the last time you bought vehicle insurance. It's akin to trading options.

You acquired insurance with your automobile when you bought it, just in case anything went wrong. You had no clue how much the repairs would cost at the time, nor did you realize how much the automobile would cost as time passed. Of course, the price may rise, but the insurance will help you protect yourself if anything goes wrong. Trading options work in the same manner.

1.3 Overview of Options

By purchasing an option, one acquires the right but not the obligation to buy or sell the underlying asset at the option's strike price on or before the expiration date. If the option holder exercises their right to buy or sell a stock before the option's expiration date, the seller is obligated to fulfill the deal. The buyer must give more to the seller to enjoy this benefit.

A "call" option grants the buyer the right to acquire a stock at a predetermined price, while a "put" option grants the buyer the option to sell a stock at the same predetermined price.

Calls and puts are both regularly traded options.

You'll need to create a "margin account" with a broker to trade options. While it is true that you will need to be a bit more financially capable to create such an account (typically a $5,000 minimum), there are several low-risk choice techniques.

Some options methods are basic, while others are more sophisticated, and some are utilized to generate revenue continuously.

Options give a lot of leverage, and trading options correctly may be less dangerous than trading the underlying stocks directly, as long as you don't misuse them.

To help you get a handle on the basics of options, I'll go over things like terminology, option types, options versus stocks, options language, and how to handle the unusual assignment scenario.

Later on, you'll learn about some of the strategies that can be used in conjunction with options to help traders and investors manage market risk in ways that aren't available when buying stocks or ETFs alone.

What are the odds of those outcomes? After all, trading in them is no more dangerous than trading the fundamental securities directly.

When done properly, options dealing may pose less risk than stock trading.

If you use option values that are unreasonably large in relation to the size of your account, you will run into problems associated with options' leverage features. However, the power aspect of options is what makes them so perilous when misused. But as with anything else, it's not necessary if you have the necessary expertise.

Margin requirements are much lower for options than for direct purchases of stocks or ETFs. All of the cash or the equivalent in other assets is required to buy a stock or exchange-traded fund (ETF), or with a credit account, about half or forty percent of the purchase price. If, however, you go the Choices route, you can expect to pay much less. In many cases, 10% or 5% of the margin is required to manage the same amount of shares. Again, you can get yourself into trouble if you overtrade or use position amounts that are excessive for your account balance. Trading options have a far higher profit potential than trading equities or ETFs.

Good methodologies for evaluating the price fluctuations of their underlying equities are required for successful options trading. Then, based on the underlying security evaluation, you may use the appropriate options strategy.

As a result, there are two components to this:

1. Recognize your alternatives and the many options and tactics available to you.

2. Having a way (or many approaches) for determining the probable direction of the stock, ETF/index for which you will be trading options.

As a result, you'll need both of them. But you'll need it anyhow if you're trading equities. You're not going to go into the market mindlessly placing orders; you're going to go into the market and trade based on your evaluation of the market or expected market direction.

Put Option

One definition of a put option is "an agreement between two parties to exchange Stock at the Strike Price on or before the Expiration Date." The holder of the put option has the sole discretion as to whether or not to sell the shares at the strike price by the expiration date. If the put buyer exercises their option, the put seller's second party must acquire shares of stock from them at the strike price.

If a stock is currently valued at $50 and you anticipate a decline to $40, you could invest $0.20 in a put option at $45 in the hopes of profiting from the drop. You can make a $4.80 per share profit if the stock declines to $40 and then you sell it for $45. Conversely, the seller of the option would be forced to buy the stock from you at $45, losing $4.80 in the process. If the share price of the underlying security never drops below $45 before the option's expiration date, the option will end worthless, costing the put buyer $0.20 and rewarding the put seller with $0.40.

Call Option

A call option is a contract requiring the parties to exchange shares of equity at a predetermined strike price and time. If the strike price is reached before the expiration date of the option, the buyer of the option has the right but not the duty to purchase the stock at the strike price. If a call option is exercised, the option's seller must transfer the underlying shares to the option's purchaser at the strike price.

If a stock is currently trading at $50, and you anticipate that it will increase to $60, you could invest $0.20 in a call option that would allow you to buy the stock at $55. Even if the stock is now worth $60, you could buy it for $55 and make a profit of $4.80 per share if it grew in value to $60. However, the person who sold you the call would be out $4.80 if they were forced to give you the stock at $55. If the stock price doesn't rise to $55 by the option's expiration date, the option is worthless, and the customer loses $0.20 while the seller keeps $0.20.

1.4 Types of Options

One can trade stocks, ETFs, indexes, futures, foreign exchange, and other underlying assets.

The main focus will be on stocks, ETFs, and indexes. Keep in mind that not all stocks, ETFs, or indexes provide options, but hundreds do give monthly options. As a result, there is a surplus compared to what is needed for effective options trading.

Options with monthly expirations can be bought and sold simultaneously regardless of when in the future those options expire. Therefore, it's possible to have a call option in July, another in August, another in September, and yet another in December.

as in the case of simultaneous buying. Options with a monthly expiration date have their last selling day as the third Friday of the month.

Expiration dates for LEAPS options can be more than a year in the future.

The acronym LEAPS, which means for "long-term options," is not easy to keep in mind. The last day to trade a LEAP is the third Friday of January because all LEAPS end the following Saturday.

Recent market developments have seen the introduction of weekly options for more than a hundred individual stocks, exchange-traded funds, and benchmarks. The principles are identical to monthly options, with the exception that weekly options expire after only a week. These options are available for trading at the same moment but have different expiration dates in different weeks in the future. Weekly options commence trading each Thursday at 9:30 a.m. Eastern Standard Time (EST) when the stock markets open. Weekly options expire at the end of trading on the following Saturday after the stock markets conclude at 4:00 p.m. Eastern Standard Time on the preceding Friday. Most weekly options are only good for four weeks.

1.5 Options and Stocks

The options' value will rise and fall in tandem with the stock's performance.

Options trade on the open market in a manner analogous to that of stock, though certain options have very light trading volumes and are best ignored.

Options can be bought and sold prior to expiration as long as the underlying stock market is available. Consequently, you can initiate or close an option transaction whenever the market is open. Holding an option holding until its expiration date is optional.

There is no set quantity of contracts that can be traded for each choice. As many options contracts as the markets are interested in buying and selling, options market builders will create a market for them.

Conversely, the number of shares that can be exchanged in a stock is capped. In contrast to equities, which do not age or expire, options contracts do.

As the equity price fluctuates, so does the option's value.

An option's price is determined by its intrinsic worth and its extrinsic value, both of which will be discussed in more detail below. Options may give authority over the same number of shares of stock for a much smaller margin.

1.6 The Options Contract

Option type, the underlying asset, strike price, expiry date, exercise mode, and contract unit are the parameters that characterize an option contract.

Types of Options

The two most common types of options are "calls" and "puts." The holder of a call option is obligated to acquire the underlying resource on or before the expiration date at a predetermined price. Holders of put options are obligated to sell the underlying asset by a specified date and price, but they are not required to do so.

Underlying Asset

Underlying Commodity Options can be purchased on a wide variety of stocks, indices, and futures contracts. The value of a stock option is determined by the number of units of stock that it entitles the holder to purchase. The value of an index option is the amount of money that would be received if the option were exercised, multiplied by the index's value (sometimes cash-settled).

Price of a Strike

When an option is exercised, the buyer or vendor of the underlying commodity is required to do so at the striking price, which is also known as the exercise price. This is the case regardless of whether the option was bought or sold in the open market.

Date of Expiration

It is the final day that the option is available.

Exercise Methodology

In the United States and Europe, people tend to favor particular types of physical training. American options can be exercised at any moment prior to their expiration date, while European options can only be done so on the expiration date itself (or, more realistically, at a certain time on any trading day before the expiration date). Because of their hybrid nature between American and European options, Bermudan options are often referred to as "early exercise" options. Asians, Russians, Zionists, Hawaiians, and Parisians are some other possibilities. On the other hand, they are associated with factors apart from exercise methodology.

Contract Unit

As the smallest tradable quantity of the underlying commodity that can be purchased or sold when an option is exercised, the contract unit is the basic unit of measurement for options. In the United States, one contract unit for individual stock options typically consists of one hundred shares of equity. When purchasing index options, this is equivalent to putting up $100 times the worth of the underlying index. Simply stated, one futures contract stands for a potential outcome in the futures market.

At a price of $3.00 per choice, the total cost to the customer is $3,100.

Traders of stock options should be cognizant of the fact that the company's actions may affect the number of contract units issued or the strike price at which the options can be purchased. While the stock price and strike price go down during an integer stock split, the number of active contracts goes up by the split factor. For example, if a stock splits 2:1, the split ratio would be 2, resulting in a reduced strike price and more options. The number of possible contracts grows while the contract unit expands if the divisor is not an integer. The contract unit would rise to 150 shares in the case of a 3-for-2 stock split, but the stock price and target price would fall by 50%. If we fix the number of active contracts, the number of contract units, and the strike price, then that figure will remain fixed forever. Recapitalizations, special payments, and rights offerings will be handled uniformly.

CHAPTER 2

Options Trading Basics

2.1 How to Get Started With Options Trading?

Exchanges of Options

Trades are done on one of the several regulated exchanges. Most options are available on many exchanges. Due to the standardized nature of option contracts, they may be traded across conversations.

The following are the eleven extant option exchanges:

- NYSE Arca Options

- BOX Options Exchange

- NASDAQ OMX PHLX

- C2 Options Exchange

- NASDAQ OMX BX

- BATS Options Exchange

- NASDAQ Options Market

- International Securities Exchange (ISE)

- NYSE Amex Options

- Chicago Board Options Exchange (CBOE)

- MIAX Options Exchange is a stock exchange that trades options.

OCC

The Options Clearing Corporation (OCC) is a financial services firm (OCC). It was established in 1973 to operate as a clearinghouse for option contracts. It is the issuer and guarantee for options and futures contracts. The OCC should reassure investors that they will settle transactions, get premiums, and complete all assignments following the rules. The Securities and Exchange Commission has authority over it (SEC).

Opening a Trading Account

Before starting trading options, you'll need to create a brokerage account. There are various brokerage firms to choose from, including full-service and cheap brokers. The kind you select is determined by the quantity of guidance you need. Discount businesses provide lower costs but no personalized guidance. All major businesses provide various online information and calculators to help you with your financial selections.

- Charles Schwab—www.schwab.com—is one of the highest-rated brokerage firms.

- www.merrilledge.com–Merrill Edge

- www.fidelity.com—Fidelity Investments

- Interactive Brokers (www.interactivebrokers.com) is an online brokerage firm.

- Trade Station (www.tradestation.com) is an online trading platform.

- TD Ameritrade (www.tdameritrade.com) TD Ameritrade (www.tdameritrade.com) TD Ameritrade (

- Options House (www.optionshouse.com) is a website where you may learn about many options.

- www.optionsxpress.com—Optionspress

- trade Monster (www.trademonster.com) is an online trading platform.

- E*Trade (www.etrade.com) is an online trading platform.

- Place Trade (http://www.placetrade.com/)

Choose between a cash account and a margin account once you've settled on a brokerage firm. The collateral in a margin account can be used as a loan to finance business transactions. You can convert your account to the cash on hand in a checking account. If you decide to open a margin account, you'll need to put down at least $2,000 to get started. In most cases, a cash account can be opened with either zero dollars or a small fee.

Margin accounts required varying sums of money and assets, depending on the Brokerage Firm. The company will send a margin call if the balance drops too low. It means you'll have to put more money into the account to meet their minimal criteria. The brokerage business will liquidate your assets if you don't do this. For this reason, you must be aware of your margin needs.

Options Agreement

Assuming you have an account set up, the next step is to execute an options agreement before you can begin trading options. Your familiarity with options trading, ability to bear the financial loss, and willingness to take on risk are all laid out in this agreement. After you've signed the dotted line at the brokerage, you'll be placed in an options acceptance tier.

Making a Purchase

Most newcomers to options trading make the mistake of thinking that all there is to it is picking which options to buy and when to sell. However, things aren't quite that straightforward. When trading options, there are four primary orders that can be placed. There are four distinct types of trades: open, close, open/close, and close/close. You can place a limit order or a market order, depending on which order type you select. As an additional step, you must allow your broker to process your order based on its specific time.

Types of Orders

The numerous types of orders are listed below:

- To open, you must first purchase. The buy-to-open order is the quickest and most common way to place an order for options. It is used to acquire an options contract to establish a new position.

- Purchase to complete the transaction. It's utilized to conclude a transaction with an established short place. You would place a purchase-to-close order It would be useful if you had temporarily sold an options contract and now wanted to close the position. Using a buy-to-close order, you can lock in your profits from the sale of options contracts and buy them back at the new, lower price. However, if the value of the options you sold short has gone up and you don't want to lose any more money, you can place a purchase order to close the order and buy back the contracts. You need to be aware of whether you have taken a short position, in which case you profit when the option's price drops and suffer a loss when the cost of the vote rises.

- Open only if you can make a sale. The purpose of this order is to open a short position in an options contract. When selling a covered call, you can use this type of order.

- Make a sale and get the deal done. The sell-to-close order will be used. The only thing that changes is the order in which options contracts are sold. The sequence is used for calls or entries.

Types of Fill Orders

One must decide how to complete an order after deciding on the type of order desired. Business, cap, stop, and stop-limit orders are some of the alternatives.

When you place a restricted order, the buy or sell price cannot be higher than the specified amount or lower than the specified amount. That way, you won't overpay for contracts or undersell your goods.

With a market order, your purchase would be completed at the going rate. Options prices fluctuate frequently, so you run the risk of buying or selling contracts at a higher or lower price than expected.

When the market price reaches the stop price, the order will be executed. The stop order and the limit order are combined in the stop-limit order.

Orders of Priority

When placing an order, please specify a time frame or duration. Day orders, all or none orders, fill or kill orders, orders good until canceled, orders good until date, and orders good until date or immediate or cancel are all examples of timing orders.

Each day's order must be either executed or canceled before the market opens.

All-or-nothing service means that orders have to be fulfilled in their entirety. If you ask your broker to buy 30 contracts of an option at a given price but he or she can only do so for 25 contracts, your request will be denied. Not like a day order, which is canceled at the end of the trading day, this one stays active until you cancel it.

Like an all-or-nothing order, a fill-or-destroy order is automatically canceled if it isn't filled immediately.

The GTC (good until canceled) order remains in effect unless and until it is canceled. Any changes you make to this order will be saved until you either cancel it or it is fulfilled.

After the specified end date, the GTD order will be canceled.

The immediate or cancel order is very similar to the fill or destroys order, with one key difference. If one order is fulfilled rapidly using this strategy but the others aren't, the latter are voided.

Options Chains: An Overview

Options chains give important information to investors who wish to trade. Real-time choice chains are available on most financial websites and brokers.

Here's a quick rundown on how to interpret a chain of options.

- All relevant information about the underlying stock, including its name, ticker symbol, exchange listing, current market price, and volume, is displayed at the top of the table.

- The columns in an options chain include: strike, symbol, last, change, bid, ask, volume, and open interest.

- Each option's strike price is listed in the first column.

- The second column contains the option's symbol. For each strike price, the chain details both call and put options (P).

- The "bid" represents the current asking price at which potential option purchasers are actively shopping. The asking price is the lowest possible price at which the seller would consider selling.

- Exchange option contracts as of that day's date are represented by the number shown.

- The open interest column displays the total number of active contracts.

Making Deals

The actual method of execution, whether you choose to trade online or over the phone, is straightforward and uniform.

Setting Up the Trade

To place a trade, you'll need the following:

- Thealternative'semblem.

- The type of option is either a put or a call option.

- The price of the strike.

- The expiry date.

- The price you're prepared to pay: Limits on the market or orders.

- Timing of orders: order of the day, delicate till full, and so on.

Order Acknowledgment

Before placing your order, double-check all details and ensure everything is correct. After you've placed your purchase, you'll get an order confirmation. The request has yet to be approved, and it may be awaiting completion.

Trade Execution

Depending on the specifics of your trade, it could take a few minutes, hours, or even days to complete your transaction.

Be Patient

Keep an eye on your positions and stick to your plan.

2.2 Benefits of Options Trading

The nicest thing about options trading is that you may benefit from the underlying asset's price movement without having to invest in it.

Investing in options is also less expensive than investing in the underlying asset. Furthermore, if you invest directly in the asset, you will have less leverage. In other words, by trading options, you have access to many more resources than you would otherwise have.

And when you put it all up, the leverage, the resources, and so on, you'll see that an investor may make more money per dollar invested than if they invested directly in the asset. Furthermore, with options, an investor may only lose a certain amount of money, which is the premium he or she has paid.

It implies you won't lose everything if you don't pay everything into the premium. It is ideal if you only want to test the waters and aren't ready to go all-in.

Another major benefit of options trading is that you may use hedging as a kind of insurance to protect yourself from excessive losses. It implies you can also protect yourself against the stock market's wild swings.

To minimize your losses, we strongly advise you to begin by hedging as much as possible.

Another benefit is that you may profit even if the stock isn't doing well. It is due to trade up, down, or sideways to enhance leverage and profits. The stock price will often decline, and you will still make a profit at the end of the day.

Furthermore, fees are far lower in options trading (which is why stockbrokers advise against it). These commissions are considerably cheaper if you go via an internet broker since they want to beat their competitors.

It also allows you to diversify your portfolio by investing in many markets. It means you may put your money into everything from agriculture to foreign exchange. Furthermore, unlike large organizations, you do not need to invest a large sum of money. All you need is a little investment to get started making money.

2.3 Volatility

Volatility is defined as the propensity for anything to vary or alter considerably. Volatility, in general, refers to the Value at which the price of a financial item increases or falls.

A financial instrument with minimal volatility has reasonably consistent pricing.

A high-volatility financial instrument, on the other hand, is prone to large price movements in either direction. We assess financial market volatility in general. As a result, when the market becomes impossible to anticipate, and prices continue to fluctuate often and fast, the market is volatile.

Volatility has a big impact on the option price. Many novice options traders overlook the ramifications, resulting in significant financial losses.

Before engaging in any transaction, including options trading, it is important to understand its volatility. Volatility is a key aspect in determining how options are evaluated and priced.

Volatility in History

Historical or statistical volatility, which is based on real data, is used to determine the option's price. Let's call it "HV" for short. The HV value represents the rate of change in the stock price. If the HV is high, the stock price has seen substantial volatility. So, in theory, at least, a stock with a high HV will experience more price swings. It's not so much a promise as a suggestion of potential motion.

Conversely, if the HV is low, it could mean that the stock price hasn't changed much, but rather has been trending in the same direction.

The historical volatility (HV) of a security's price can be used to estimate how much that price will fluctuate in the future, but it cannot be used to predict a trend.

HV is typically calculated after a set time period, such as a week, month, or year.

Implied Volatility

Implied volatility, or IV, is an important concept for options traders to keep in mind. In contrast to historical volatility, which is measured by HV, expected volatility is calculated by IV.

The expected volatility (IV) of a security is a measure of its potential for future price swings. Many novice traders ignore intrinsic value (IV) when calculating the value of an option in favor of more intuitive metrics like profit (the spread between the strike price and the stock price) and time left until expiration.

Variables such as the stock and strike prices, time until expiration, interest rate, and HV can all be factored into an option's intrinsic value calculation. As the implied volatility (IV) of an option increases, the price of the underlying stock may increase as well. Because in theory, your profits will be higher whenever there are large swings in the underlying stock price. The intrinsic value (IV) of an option can cause its value to change even if the stock price remains unchanged.

So, for instance, there are rumors that ABC is working on a new product and will announce it soon. The implied volatility (IV) of options on stock ABC may be quite high because of the high likelihood of large volatility in the underlying stock price. Even if the news is true and the stock price rises, the product may still fail to impress its target market, leading to a precipitous decline in share value. Since investors are likely to wait for the announcement before buying or selling stocks, the stock price may not change in this scenario. As a result, rather than the stock price changes, the extrinsic value of both puts and calls will increase. An example of a potential way in which IV affects the price of an option is this.

At-the-money call options are purchased when the buyer anticipates a significant increase in the stock price as a result of the news. If ABC had been announced and accepted, stock prices would have skyrocketed, and the call options' intrinsic value would have increased significantly.

2.4 Variety of Options and Their Styles

The ways appear in a wide variety of forms, sizes, and shapes. In the broadest sense, options can be broken down into two primary categories: calls and puts. In addition to purchasing the option, a buyer of a call option also has the option to buy the underlying asset, while a buyer of a put option has the option to sell the asset. Common practise classifies alternatives according to whether they are American or European in style. In addition to this distinct difference, the location of the contracts is irrelevant; rather, the important consideration is the availability of the parties to carry out their obligations at the appropriate time. There is more detail about the distinctions in the following sections.

Calls

When an investor holds a call option, he or she has the contractual right but not the obligation to buy the underlying asset at a predetermined future date and price. You should buy a call option if you believe that the value of the underlying asset will increase within a specified time frame. Calls have a termination date and, subject to the terms of the contract, the underlying asset may be purchased at any time prior to or on the termination date.

Puts

One could say that put options are the polar opposite of call options. Puts give the owner the right, at a later date and for a specified price, to sell the underlying commodity. Thus, if you thought the underlying commodity's price would fall, you'd make a wise investment by purchasing a put option. Like phone calls, this exchange of information is time-limited.

American Style

When it comes to options, the phrase "American style" refers to the terms of the contracts, not where they are purchased or sold. Options contracts contain an expiry date after which the owner can purchase.

opportunity to exercise at any point before the contract's expiry date. The owner of an American-style contract will benefit from greater freedom.

European Design

Owners of options contracts of a European-type do not have the same level of freedom as owners of contracts in the American manner. If you hold a contract of the European variety, for a contract.

Options That Are Traded on an Exchange

It is the most frequent choice, often known as listed options. Any options contract posted on a public trading exchange is referred to as "Exchanged Traded." Anyone may buy and sell them.

Options Available Over-the-Counter

Because "Over-the-Counter" (OTC) options can only be traded on OTC markets, the general population has a more difficult time gaining access to them. In most cases, they take the form of bespoke contracts that feature conditions that are more complex than those of standard ETFs.

Underlying Security Option Type

When people talk about options, they usually mean stock options, in which the underlying asset is stock in a publicly-traded corporation. While these are the most prevalent, there

are a variety of additional variants in which the underlying security is different. The most prevalent of these are the following:

- **Stock Options:** These contracts have shares in a publicly-traded corporation as their underlying asset.

- Stock options and index options are very similar financial instruments; however, in the case of the latter, the underlying investment is an index such as the S&P 500.

- Currency options and foreign exchange options give the owner the right to buy or sell a specific currency at a specified exchange rate.

- In the case of futures options, the underlying security is a futures contract. The owner of a futures option simply gains the opportunity to take part in the selected futures contract.

- A physical commodity or a commodity futures contract could form the basis of a commodity options contract.

- Options in a "basket" are a type of derivative contract based on a group of assets rather than a single one. Stocks, currencies, commodities, and other financial instruments are all examples of such assets.

Expiration Type Option

One way to categorize contracts is by the time period in which the contract holder must exercise their right to buy or sell the underlying asset in accordance with the terms of the contract. Some contracts only offer one possible termination date, while others provide several. Although most options traders won't need this knowledge, it might help some of them better understand the terminology. Here are some examples of contracts and when they typically run out:

Regular Options:

- These options are the standardized expiry cycles that are supplied with options contracts. Regular options are the most common type of option. When you purchase a contract of this kind, you will have the option to choose from at least four different months in which the contract will expire. The limitations that were placed on when options could first be introduced to the market and on when they could be exchanged are the root cause of these expiration cycles. The expiration periods might be a little difficult to understand, but all you need to know.

- **Weekly Options:** These choices, which were initially introduced for the first time in 2005 and are also referred to as weeklies, The concept behind weekly options is the same as that behind regular options; the main difference is that weekly options have a substantially shorter time to expiration.

- **Quarterly Options:** called "quarterlies," these securities are listed on exchanges for a period of four quarters and one additional quarter. When compared to standard contracts, which typically end on the third Friday of the month, quarterly agreements typically end on the last day of the month.

- **Long-Term Expiration Anticipation Assets (LEAPS):** Terms offered on a broad variety of underlying securities and are often referred to as LEAPS. LEAPS always expire in January, although they may be purchased with three-year expiration dates.

Stock Options for Employees

Employees are offered contracts tied to the equity of the company they work for, in the form of stock options. They're often given to new hires as an incentive to work for the company, a reward for their hard work, or some combination of those things.

Options Costing Real Money

The underlying asset is not transferred during the exercise or settlement of a cash-settled contract. Instead, the party that does not share in the profit is required to pay the party that does share in the profit a sum of money equal to that party's share of the profit. This kind of contract is typically used when transferring the underlying asset to the other party would be difficult or costly. Find more details on Cash Settled Options on their specialized website.

Alternatives That Are Out of the Ordinary

A contract that has been tailored with more complicated clauses is referred to as an exotic option. They're also known as non-Standardized choices. Several exotic contracts are available, many of which are only accessible via OTC marketplaces.

However, certain exotic contracts are gaining popularity among mainstream investors and are published on public exchanges.

- **Barrier Options:** These contracts' payout to the holder of the underlying security reaches a pre-determined price (or does not, depending on the contract's conditions).

- **Choose Options:** These options are called "Chooser" because they enable the contract's owner to pick whether the agreement is a call or a put when a certain date is reached.

- **Compound Options:** These are options with another options contract as the underlying security.

- **Look Back Options:** This form of contract enables the owner to exercise the security at a good price obtained throughout the contract's period rather than having a strike price.

CHAPTER 3
Options Trading Fundamentals

Fundamental analysis is a method of reviewing stocks that seeks to measure their intrinsic worth. From the general economy and trade dynamics to the financial health and supervision of different organizations, fundamental analysts are interested in various topics. Fundamental analysts scrutinize all aspects of a company's operations, including earnings, costs, assets, and liabilities.

3.1 Charts

Even though we can know what a piece of news implies, and we'll see how the market adjusts to it, the charting is more relevant to options traders than just about every other repository of material. Whenever a price change occurs, it is initially reported on the charts, which impacts how we trade it. In technical analysis of stock (as distinguished by quantitative research), the most important aspect is reading charts, which involves observing price activity, and tonnage action, and assessing structures on the charts.

Reading Charts

To Spot Patterns and Build Long-Term Reference Lines, Traders Use Charts

Prices do not show on charts in a distributed direction. Through the duration, they organize spontaneously into easily distinguishable shapes like maxima, trend lines, and times of consolidation, among other things. Traders commonly draw lines on charts to depict highs and lows over time. These lines include trading channels, support and resistance flags, pennants, cup and handles, and similar symbols. These lines assist traders in selecting methods and assist them in selecting entry and exit positions

Example

Upon the chart, you will see a "conduit" (white lines) that creates a favorable environment for "swing trading."

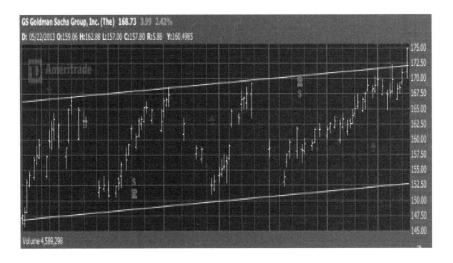

Charts Provide Trends That Traders May Utilize to Make Informed Decisions

The ideal guideline lets the charts guide you to the most appropriate plan. Bull Put Securities are particularly attractive to stocks that have been on an upswing for a lengthy period. The use of Butterfly Spreads or short Straddles might be beneficial to traders who trade in a narrow range of prices. Swing traders may trade a "channel" by using alternative techniques such as Long Puts and Long Calls, similar to long puts and long calls. If a stock "fills the gap," then pick the transaction that best allows for that to happen, then close the deal after the gap has been filled with the stock in question. When option premiums on a stock inflate before earnings are developed, trading strategies allow traders to benefit from the "volatility crush" and increase their profits. Once the trading range has been determined, it is possible to make regular revenue by selling puts and calls that are well out of the money.

Charts Direct Traders Toward Bigger Earnings in the Following Ways

Once techniques have been established, charts may be used to identify areas of optimum profitability. Because 550 indicated major resistance, this chart of AAPL suggested a goal of $550 to close a gap in the market. During the first quarter of 2014, the stock increased from $505 to 550, and we could close out our stake successfully. The stock then plummeted as resistance overpowered momentum, and the stock began to decline. The chart provided us with the numbers for our entrance and departure points.

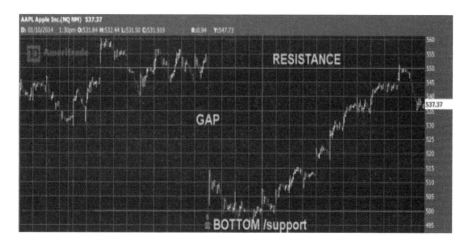

3.2 Charts Have Specific Characteristics That Help You Make Money

Here are some popular chart patterns that practically everyone notices and that can assist you in making better trading decisions in the future.

Anyone who understands these patterns will be more effective in their trading.

Range

In terms of stock action over the moment, how wide is the spread? You will often discover two important turning places, one on the way up and one on the lowest setting, or one on the way up and one down. The yellow dashed line shows YTD (year-to-date) angular values. The following is a year-to-date analysis for MA, which shows the stock in a lengthy sideways band.

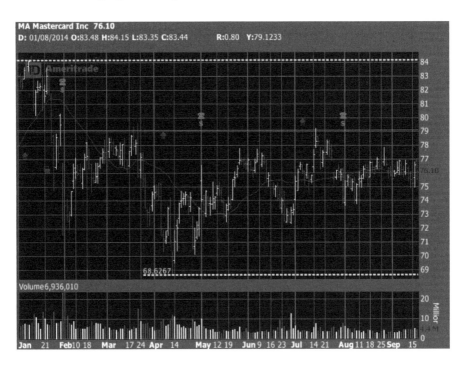

Trend

Is the stock's price trending upward, downward, or sideways over time? There are many significant turning sites throughout the range. Each one of them indicates a reversal in the stock's trend. To identify a trend, we draw a simple white line along the bottoms or peaks of the price action chart. The "bearish" trend is characterized by lower lows and lower highs, whereas higher lows and higher highs characterize the "bullish" trend. Traders will often notice that the tails of price activity follow these lines predictably. Do you want to know if the stock is heading up, down, or sideways? When a trend comes to an end, does it come to a halt like a Hawaiian beach or an iceberg in the Arctic? Here is an example of MTD displaying two trends. The beginning of a new trend occurs at the same moment when the price crosses above the downward line.

Relationship to the Moving Average

In your "Technical Studies," first ensure that "Linear Function" is chosen from the drop-down menu. On your pricing charts, it will appear as a red line. Is there a relationship between the stock's price and its 30-day moving average?

Indicators such as the Trend line are among the most often used on charts. A bullish trend is verified when a stock trades consistently above the average for a long period.A bearish trend is validated when a stock trades consistently below the standard, and a horizontal trend is proven when a stock creeps horizontally along with the average.

On this particular stock of GOOGL, we can observe the stock trading above the red MA (30), then below, then above again, and then alternating between the two sides in a sideways movement. Not many stock charts are as straightforward as this one, but it is simple to trade on.

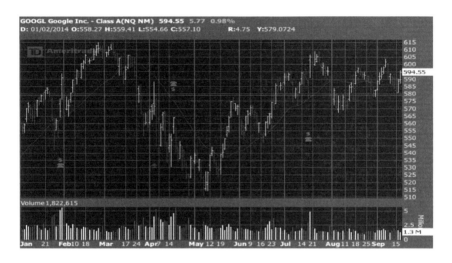

Gaps

Is there a spot on the chart with nothing but a blank space? Take a check at your elected charts to determine any big discrepancies between them. Are there any gaps on the chart, and do the gaps eventually fill up? Generally speaking, you will discover them related to 1) changes in trend and 2) earnings reports or important news announcements, which may move up or down at a price. These are very beneficial to options traders since they inform us that buyers and sellers have swiftly reset their price expectations, which is really important information. Identifying and filling up the gaps. Gaps in the market are among the most dependable indicators that a stock's direction has altered. Traders' determination to not reverse a new downtrend or upswing will signal the beginning of a new trend. Examine the following chart from PCLN, and you will see multiple affirmative gaps. The evidence is more compelling if the gap exceeds the Moving Average line. On the chart for PCLN, various gaps prove the presence of the stock.

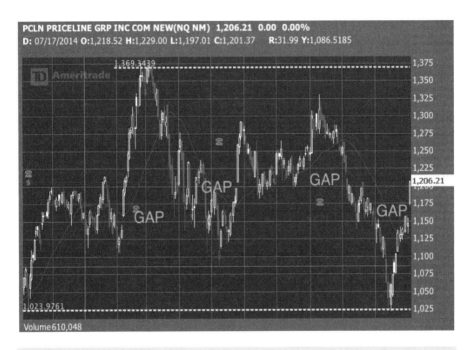

3.3 Option Pricing

The theoretical basis for determining the premium attached to an options contract is the probability that the contract will expire in the money (ITM) at the time the premium is calculated. Simply put, option pricing theory provides a valuation of an option's fair value that traders can use as part of their trading strategy.

In order to assign a hypothetical value to an option, pricing models take into account a number of different variables, including the current market price, the strike price, volatility, interest rate, and the remaining time until expiration. Some common approaches to determining an option's worth include the Black-Scholes model, binomial option pricing, and Monte-Carlo simulation.

Understanding Pricing Option Theory

Assigning a monetary value to the probability of an option being exercised or being in the money at the time of its expiration is the primary goal of a well-functioning options market. Theoretical recoverable amounts for options are typically calculated using mathematical models that take into account a number of different factors, including the intrinsic asset's price (for example, the price of a stock), the option's exercise price, volatility, and time to expiration (the number of days between the calculation date and the option's exercise date). Options time to expiration, or the number of days between the date of calculation and the option's expiration, is another widely-used variable. The options pricing methodology develops a number of risk factors or sensitivities as a consequence of such inputs. These risk factors and sensitivities are collectively referred to as an option's "Greeks." The Greeks provide a method for marketers to utilize in order to evaluate how responsive a deal is to price increases, variations in volatility, and the shifting of the seasons.

The Black Scholes Formula

There are numerous approaches to estimating the worth of an option's payoff, the most well-known being the Black-Scholes model. The formula for the prototype is the share price multiplied by the normal probability function of the stochastic process. The stochastic process is the source of this function. The cumulative standard normal distribution is multiplied by the net present value (NPV) of the strike price to derive the amount to be deducted from the total. To avoid including this sum in the previous calculation's results, we will modify them.

$$C = S_t N(d_1) - Ke^{-rt} N(d_2)$$

where:

$$d_1 = \frac{ln\frac{S_t}{K} + (r + \frac{\sigma_r^2}{2})\,t}{\sigma_s\,\sqrt{t}}$$

and

$$d_2 = d_1 - \sigma_s\,\sqrt{t}$$

where:

$C =$ Call option price

$S =$ Current stock (or other underlying) price

$K =$ Strike price

$r =$ Risk-free interest rate

$t =$ Time to maturity

$N =$ A normal distribution

It's possible that the mathematics necessary to solve a differential equation, a fundamental component of the Black-Scholes formula, will be challenging and nerve-wracking. To incorporate Black-Scholes modeling into your approach, you do not need to be a mathematician or even have a basic understanding of mathematics. For the convenience of traders and investors, a number of online possibility calculators are accessible. Many of today's trading platforms include in-depth tools for options analysis, such as indicators and workbooks that perform calculations and provide option pricing values. These tools are included in the vast majority of trading platforms.

3.4 Options Order

Market orders, limit trading, and stop-loss commands are the three most often used forms of orders.

An order to buy or sell a security at the current market price on the same day is called a "market order." Although this type of order guarantees fulfillment, the exact quantity ordered cannot be specified. But traders must be aware that the last traded price of a stock is not necessarily the price at which a market order will be filled.

Instructing your broker to buy or sell a security at a specified price or better is what a "limit order" is. A purchase limit order can be fulfilled only at or below the restriction price, while a sale restriction order can be fulfilled only at or above the limit. An example transaction would be an investor's desire to purchase ABC stock for no more than $10 per share. The investor may submit a limit order to buy this quantity of ABC stock at $10 or less.

A "stop order," also known as a "stop-loss order," is an order to buy or sell stock at a specified price (the "stop price") if the stock's price rises to that level before the order's expiration. When the stop price is reached, the stop order will automatically become a market order.

In this scenario, a buy-stop order is placed and executed at a price higher than the current market price. When shorting a stock, investors use a buy-stop order to limit their losses and protect their profits. A sell-stop order can be set for a price lower than the current market price. A sell-stop order is used by investors to limit their loss or protect their gain on a stock.

3.5 Trade Signal

A recommendation to buy or sell an asset based on the findings of an analysis used as a trading reference signal. These can include technical indicators and, if available, economic data, as well as mathematical algorithms based on market behavior.

How Trade Signals Works

Trade signals may be generated from several inputs originating from various disciplines. Although technical analysis is often the most important component and inputs.

Beyond basic buy and sell signals, trade signals may also be used to change a portfolio, such as deciding when it may be advantageous to invest more in one area, such as technology, while lessening one's exposure to another, such as consumer staples. For bond traders, selling one maturity and purchasing another maturity might provide indications for modifying the length of their portfolios, allowing them to change the duration of their portfolios. Finally, it may aid in asset class allocation, such as distributing funds across equities, bonds, and precious metals, among others.

There is no absolute maximum on how comprehensive a trading signal may be created. Managing a basic signal generator and occasionally testing it to determine which components need tweaking or replacing is significantly more convenient in practice than managing a complex signal generator.

CHAPTER 4

Mistakes to Avoid in Options Trading

This chapter will teach you about some of the most typical options trading blunders, which will help you make better-educated trading choices in the future.

It is natural for beginner options traders to feel overwhelmed when they first start. One of the advantages of trading options is that it provides several different methods to profit from what you predict will happen to the underlying investment in the future. However, one of the trade-offs for the luxury of such a wide selection is a higher likelihood of making mistakes. Ultimately, the purpose of this essay is to raise awareness of some of the most prevalent options trading blunders to assist options traders in making better-educated trading choices.

4.1 Your Strategy Does Not Correspond to Your Outlook

One of the most crucial skills to have while learning how to trade options is to construct an outlook for what visitors perceive might happen. Trend analysis, fundamental analysis, and even a combination of these two are the most typical beginning platforms for forming an investment view. Market action (mostly volume and price) is interpreted on a chart, and areas of support, resistance, and trends are identified to find new buy and sell opportunities. When conducting fundamental analysis, it is necessary to examine a company's financial accounts, performance statistics, and current business trends to develop a viewpoint on its value. When you create an outlook, you include a directional bias and a time range for how long you anticipate it will take to implement the ideas you've generated.

You should carefully examine various options and processes to enhance that the strategy you choose is geared to enjoy the benefits of the perspective you anticipate. Getting acquainted with numerous tactics through Fidelity's Options Strategy Guide is a good approach to familiarize yourself with them and choose which one is most fit for your scenario.

4.2 Selecting the Incorrect Expiration Date

Just as with methodologies, while choosing an expiration date, individuals are confronted with the problem of having a large number of options to choose from. The good news is that if you build a strategy, choosing the appropriate expiration date will almost always fall into place automatically. A basic checklist can be useful in assisting you in determining the optimal expiration date for your situation.

Most position allocation errors are caused by two main emotional states: fear and greed. If you are overconfident in your selections, you may end up trading with a position size that is excessive for your margin requirement. A deal that goes even against the forecast may result in a crushing loss, and you may find yourself in this situation. On the other hand, you may be like certain dealers who deal in incredibly small quantities. You will not be penalized for trading a little size, but you will lose out on a potential material return.

4.3 Selecting Wrong Position Sizes

- You are taking a percentage of your account worth on the line.

- The percentages are as follows: 1 %, 2 %, 3 %, etc.

- Make use of a regular cash amount.

- $100, $500, $1,000, and so forth.

Finally, while determining the magnitude of the trade, you should be satisfied with the amount of capital you will lose if the trade does not turn out in your favor. In an ideal situation, the trade size would be substantial enough to be significant to the account but modest enough that you wouldn't lose sleep over the decision.

4.4 Ignoring the Possibility of Volatility

It is critical to understand if implied volatility is reasonably strong or weak, even though this evidence is used to consider the price of an option premium. When determining which option strategy is most appropriate for your outlook, knowing whether the premium is outrageous or inexpensive is critical information to consider. Alternatively, if the options are relatively affordable, it may be more advantageous to consider debit techniques; conversely, if the options are highly expensive, it may be more advantageous to consider credit tactics.

4.5 Not Using Probability

When selecting whether or not to place a trade, it is critical to consider the probability associated with your strategy. The ability to put into perspective what is statistically likely to happen is vital for determining whether or not your risk/reward ratio is reasonable. It is critical to remember that probability does not have a directional bias.

Given the existing circumstances, it is just the statistical probability of the price being at a specific level on the evaluation date.

4.6 Focusing on Expiration Graph

As a trader, it is critical to regularly assess the amount of risk/reward you are putting on the table and determine whether or not it is still appropriate for your particular account. Concentrating solely on the expiration graph of your holdings does not reveal how much risk you are currently carrying or how much risk you will be carrying in the future.

You may examine how your position will react to trading activity not only presently but on any day in the foreseeable up until the expiration date by using the Profit/Loss Calculator tool.

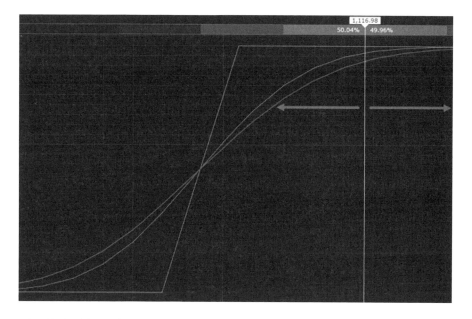

The light blue picture indicates the position at the time of termination, the dark blue line represents the position today, and the orange line indicates the position at a future date that has been chosen. As seen in this illustration, the narrow vertical bar has been shifted to the present market price level. The portion at which it intersects with the other lines indicates that many gains and losses were made on the deal at that time.

As the position now stands in this example, you've already realized most of your profits. You have a considerable amount of room on the downside to realize the biggest loss possible at expiration if the position swings in the opposite direction. You may question yourself at this stage if the probable downside risk is worth maintaining the trade to earn the maximum profit.

You can think about what would happen if the position made a significant move in either direction during the next several days or weeks. Even if it continues to rise in value, you would still profit, but the amount would be insignificant compared to what you have already earned. On the other hand, if the market takes a severe downward turn, you may find yourself losing a significant amount of the profits you've already gained. The risk/reward ratio has shifted at this point in the deal, and it may go unnoticed if you are solely concerned with the expiration date.

4.7 Not Having a Proper Plan

One of the first tasks to prevent typical trading blunders is to develop a solid trading strategy.

How much money are you inclined to dedicate at risk with each trade?

- What strategy will you use to identify opportunities in the marketplace?

- When do you intend to begin working in the industry?

- What is your plan for getting out of this situation?

As previously said, fear and greed might cause you to make irrational judgments that you would not typically consider. The primary advantage of having an investment plan is that it decouples these desires and impulses from overall trading decisions. It also results in a technique that is straightforward to replicate. Having the ability to spot weaknesses in the trades you make and learn from your mistakes is critical for success in the stock market and for learning from your failures. Without a plan, it becomes extremely difficult to progress as a trader and maintain a positive attitude.

BOOK 3

OPTION TRADING BASIC STRATEGIES

CHAPTER 1

Candlesticks and Market Trends

1.1 Candlesticks

Open, high, low, and close prices for the day are shown in a candlestick chart. The "real body" of the candlestick is its main component.

This real body represents the range of prices that occurred during the trading session in question. A lower close than open is expected if the actual body is covered in a black sealant. Due to the absence of a true body, we can infer that the closing price exceeded the opening price.

A trader's trading platform will allow for the customization of these hues. The opposite of a green up candle is typically a red down candle, and vice versa for a white green candle.

Candlestick Patterns for Beginners

Rising and falling prices are what give rise to candlesticks. In spite of how seemingly random price swings can seem, they often establish patterns that can be used by traders for analysis and profit. There is a wide variety of candlestick styles available. Here is an example to help you get started.

Patterns are identified as either bullish or bearish. Patterns that are bullish suggest that prices will rise while patterns that are bearish suggest that prices will fall. Because candlestick patterns are merely price trends and not guarantees, they are not always reliable.

As a method of technical analysis, candlestick charts incorporate information from various time periods into a single price bar. In contrast to the more common open-high, low-close bars, or the straight lines connecting the prices at the end of the day, these bars have a higher closing value. When used correctly, candlesticks can be used to predict where prices will go in the future. An accurate color system has been applied to this technological tool that was developed in Japan in the eighteenth century and is still in use by rice vendors in the modern day. Several different colors are used to create its vivid appearance.

In 1991, with the publication of his best-selling book "Japanese Candlestick Charting Strategies," Steve Nison introduced Western audiences to candlestick patterns.

Hundreds of these patterns, with names like "bearish dark cloud cover," "evening star," and "three black crows," are now common knowledge to traders. Single bar formations, such as the Doji and the hammer, have been used by both long- and short-side trading strategies.

Reliability of Candlestick Patterns

There is no universally accepted norm for the appearance of candlestick patterns. Hedge funds and the algorithms they use to evaluate investments are to blame for the decline in reliability that has accompanied their meteoric rise. In order to compete with regular investors and seasoned fund managers who use strategies commonly found in popular literature related to technical analysis, these well-funded players rely on lightning-fast execution.

Financial services firms employ technological means to encourage customers to seek out extremely bullish or bearish outcomes. We call this a "bait and switch" for lack of a better term. Persistently appearing reliable patterns, as well as those on the opposite end of the spectrum, suggest the potential for both short-term and long-term financial gains.

The following five candlestick patterns are extremely useful for forecasting future price movement and its direction. The price bars around each one serve as a forecast for whether prices will go up, down, or stay the same. Furthermore, they have dual temporal constraints:

Whether they are looking at an intraday, daily, weekly, or monthly chart, they are limited to working within the chart's boundaries.

Their strength rapidly drops by three to five bars after the pattern has been completed. This happens very quickly.

1. Three line

It tends to turn three black candlesticks within the same downturn. Each bar's low is lower than the last. The previous print is also the fourth bar's bottom. Bulkowski claims this regression accurately predicts rising spending 83% of the time.

Three Line Strike

2. Two Black Gapping

An uptrend's bearish two-black gapping continuation pattern consists of a gap down followed by two black bars with lower lows. If this trend holds, the decline will deepen, possibly touching off a broader economic downturn. According to Bulkowski, there is a 68% chance that prices will go down if this pattern continues.

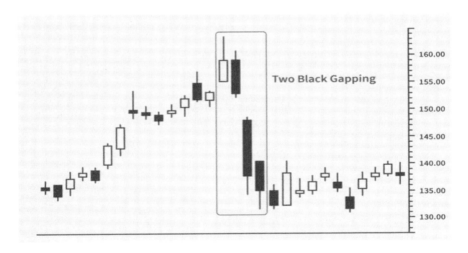

Two Black Gapping

3. Three Black Crows

This pattern indicates that a bearish trend reversal is imminent. According to this pattern, the decline will likely artificially depress lows, which could potentially initiate a wider-scale depression. The worst possible form begins at a new high because it prevents buyers from taking advantage of momentum moves (point A on the chart). This pattern has a projection performance of 78%, according to Bulkowski, and it forecasts lower costs.

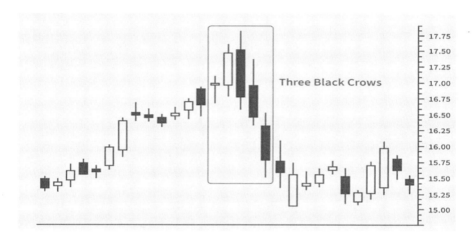

4. Evening Star

Bearish evening star regression pattern was initiated by a massive white bar. This pattern is responsible for continuing an uptrend to a new peak. On the following bar, the market gaps broaden, but there are no new buyers who enter the market, which results in a candlestick with a narrow range. According to Bulkowski, this structure has an accuracy record of 72% when it comes to predicting that prices will go down.

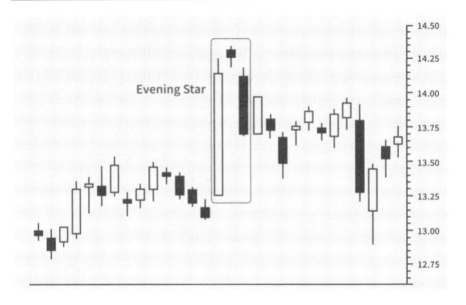

5. *Abandoned Baby*

After a string of black candles has produced lower lows, the bullish abandoned baby reversion structure will begin to take shape at the bottom of a recession. On the next bar, the market gaps are moving in a downward direction; however, there are no new sellers entering the scene, which results in a restricted range of Doji candlesticks with the same starting and closing prices. The pattern is concluded by the appearance of a positive divergence on the third candle, which suggests that the recovery will continue as a result of the implementation and may even kick off a more significant price increase. According to Bulkowski's research, this pattern has a prognostic performance of 49.73% when it comes to anticipating price increases.

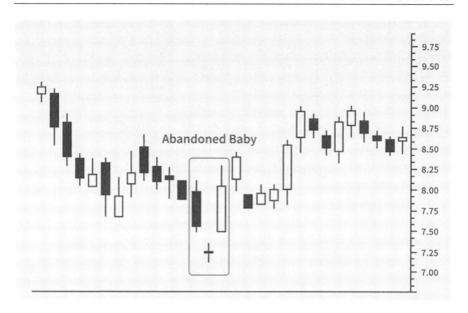

1.2 Trend

An uptrend is a sequence of higher lows typically (but not always) followed by higher highs.

Prices usually follow a trend (upward or downward) or move sideways. The following graph shows a substantial upward trend in the price till April 2012.

Between those peaks, you'll observe a drop that ends at the solid horizontal line. After the second peak, the price continues to decline by over $70 (about 10%) in a single month after the bottom has been surpassed downward.

You'll also see that the double top happens after a big trend that can be tracked on this chart back to the start of the series in December 2011.

The Double Tops Rule

So far, we've met three of the criteria:

a. A double top

b. A broken uptrend with a downward reversal (mid-May)

c. The most recent important bottom has been broken to the downside (mid-May)

You may choose from the following options:

- When the trend line is broken, exit your long position, and when the bottom is breached, exit your long position.

Triple tops follow the same rules as double tops. One of the following is a good place to start:

a. A triple top

b. An uptrend that has been broken and is now reversing to the downside (typically after the second top).

c. The most recent important bottom has been broken to the downside.

You may choose from the following options:

- When the trend line is broken, exit your long position and enter a short position.

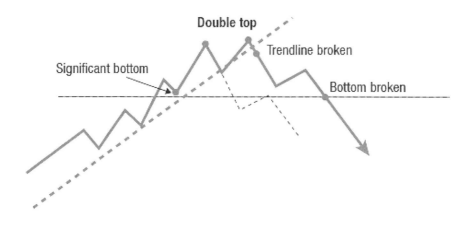

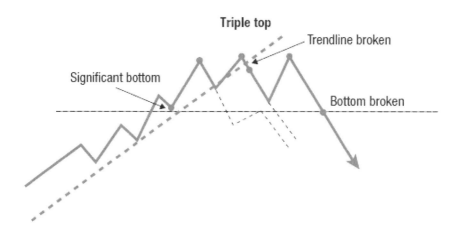

Double tops and triple tops summary

What the patterns mean.	• Weakness in the stock if it breaks down through the trendline after the second or third top.
What to do.	• Sell all holdings on breakdown through trendline. • Consider buying puts and/or selling the stock short.
How to identify the pattern.	• Two or three peaks (tops). • Broken upward trendline. • Reversal breaking down through latest significant bottom.
What is the cause?	• Lack of conviction in stock price appreciating beyond previous high.

Triple Bottoms and Double Bottoms

These are the opposites of double and triple tops. The chart indicates that the (stock) price was not weak enough to go through a prior low. It also has the power to break through the prior high point. It is seen as a strength, indicating that a price increase is inevitable.

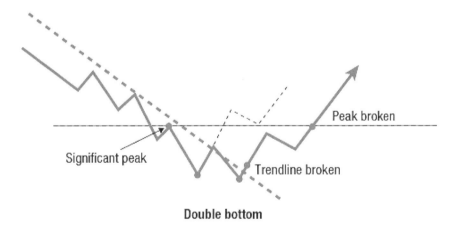

Double bottom

94

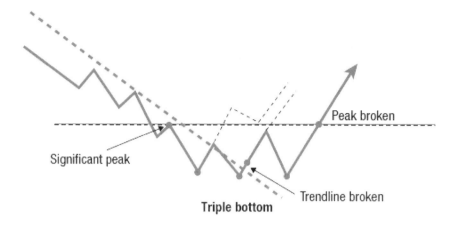

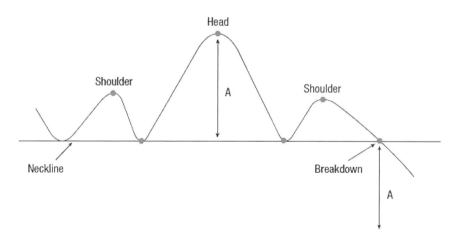

Head and Shoulder

When a peak (head) is sandwiched between two lower peaks, it forms a head and shoulders pattern (shoulders). In logical words, the chart indicates that the (stock) price lacked the power to climb beyond either of the previous highs.

Head and shoulders summary

What the pattern means.	• Possible weakness in the stock if it breaks the support line (neckline).
What to do.	• Sell all holdings on breakdown and consider buying puts and/or selling the stock short.
How to identify the pattern.	• From the neckline, a pattern develops as shown here. • First shoulder, head, second shoulder, followed by breakdown below the neckline.
What is the cause?	• A breakdown below the support line (neckline) of the stock. • One of the most reliable of the major reversal patterns.

Reverse Head and Shoulder

When a bottom (reverse head) is sandwiched between two higher bottoms, it forms a reverse shoulders and reverse head. This chart indicates that the (stock) price has the power to climb through any of the previous lows. It is seen as a strength, and a price increase of at least the distance

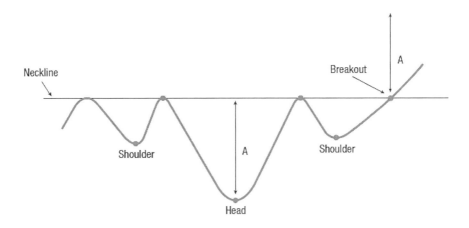

Reverse head and shoulders summary

What the pattern means.	• Possible strength in the stock if it breaks up through the resistance line (neckline).
What to do.	• Consider entering into a bullish position by buying the stock or calls.
How to identify the pattern.	• From the neckline a pattern develops as shown here. • First reverse shoulder, head, second shoulder, followed by breakout above the neckline.
What is the cause?	• A breakout above the support line (neckline) of the stock. • One of the most reliable of the major reversal patterns.

CHAPTER 2
Financial Leverages

2.1 What Is Leverage?

Traders and investors frequently employ the powerful strategy of leverage to multiply the impact of their capital. In the options market, you can leverage your investment with the help of options contracts. There is a leverage factor connected with options. When deciding how many contracts you can buy, this factor is applied to your money, and it rises as the contract's price rises. The terms "multiplier" and "leverage factor" are often used by traders.

When trading options, leverage may help you enhance your purchasing power. It means you may effectively manage more prominent positions with less cash, and the profits can be enormous when the transaction goes in your favor.

2.2 Why Is Leverage Riskier?

Leverage is another big issue to be mindful of. Because options are just a contract and do not cost as much as stock, they see disproportionately bigger percentage price increases due to the significantly more costly underlying stock's modest price fluctuations. The great advantage of this is that it produces significant percentage returns even if the underlying stock only moves a tiny bit in the desired direction. The disadvantage is that if the stock moves even a tiny amount in the incorrect direction, it wipes out the whole investment. It isn't generally a worry for novices, or it shouldn't be, since the risk is mostly shown by trading too big a position size. However, you should be aware that as useful as leverage is, it can also be a double-edged sword, so be mindful that leverage is a danger that must be managed. Keeping your position size minimal is a simple method to eliminate or reduce this degree of risk.

Finally, we know that options have a temporal value (extrinsic value) in addition to their intrinsic value (in the money value), which is a double-edged sword. Time decay is a headwind for option purchasers since it reduces the option's value over time. As a result, the trade becomes more reliant on higher stock price movement to break even. It operates as a tailwind for option writers since it enables them to earn from consistent premium revenue regardless of whether the stock rises or not.

2.3 The Benefits of Leverage in Options Trading

Options exchanges are crucial in guaranteeing sufficient stocks on which to base options contracts. Some of the most important functionalities of an options exchange are listed below (VAIDYA, 2017).

Liquidity

The most important role of options exchanges is guaranteeing that options contracts have available markets. The markets guarantee that option holders may exercise their options and that enough buyers can acquire them. Traders seek ways to boost their profit margins, and liquidity may help them do so. Unlike other instruments such as shares, which need liquidity, options contracts have a time limit. Liquidity is mostly a result of the presence of market makers.

Gauging a Country's Economy

The condition of an options market may provide us with reliable information about a country's economic position. Our shares are the most prevalent underlying assets on which traders base their options. The current economic circumstances continually influence the share values of different firms. Share prices will rise if the nation is prospering, and they will fall if the country is suffering market collapse. As a result, the options exchanges are crucial in ensuring that traders have a sense of their country's economy. Stocks represent the economy's pulse, accurately indicating a country's economic status.

Pricing of Securities

Regarding underlying assets, options traders have a large selection to pick from. The value of an underlying asset, on the other hand, is decided by the options market and the dynamics of demand and supply. Financial securities issued by successful businesses are worth more than those issued by moderately successful businesses. Securities valuation is critical not only for traders but also for governments. Governments tax revenues from options trading; therefore, they must first determine the value of the securities.

Transactional Security

Traders want to know that they can trust all parties with whom they are doing business. As a result, an options exchange transaction requires verifying that the participants are trustworthy. For one thing, most options contracts are based on the financial assets of publicly traded corporations, which are bound by strict laws and regulations. Therefore, the trader may feel safe while dealing with other parties. To prevent traders from making decisions based on a lack of knowledge, the options markets should disclose all important information on options contracts and assets.

Allowing for Speculation

Securities speculation is necessary to maintain a healthy balance of demand and supply for securities. Many traders make money only by taking speculative risks. They have honed their ability to predict price movements. Options exchanges give traders the resources and tools they need to speculate on the performance of assets, enabling them to profit.

Encourages a Culture of Investing

Options exchanges are crucial in encouraging people to invest in valuable securities like stocks rather than unproductive assets like precious metals. Traders may choose from a broad choice of underlying assets to base their options contracts. A robust saving and investing culture is essential for economic development.

The Continuous Market for Securities

Traders may base their options on a broad selection of underlying assets on options exchanges, and they can swap from one investment to the next if there are any concerns. In contrast to stock purchases, you are left with the repercussions of bad judgments.

Formation of Capital

Options exchanges encourage the pooling of resources and their redistribution. The interactions result in a win-win scenario for both parties.

When a company's stock is publicly traded, it raises funds, and its securities serve as the underpinning. On the other hand, traders stand to gain from option contracts' great earning potential and minimal capital needs. As a result, options exchanges are crucial in guaranteeing that the parties can create cash.

Companies in Charge of Surveillance

A trader who has the misfortune of dealing with dodgy businesses risks losing all of their money. Options exchanges make it difficult for unethical businesses to destabilize the market. Publicly-traded corporations, for example, are required to present appropriate paperwork and meet particular performance benchmarks to improve investor trust.

Companies that refuse to comply with exchanges are barred from participating in the market.

Monetary and Fiscal Policies

The government's fiscal and monetary policies must not harm the participants in the financial industry. Options exchanges make developing and implementing crucial regulations that will control financial markets easier.

Canalization of Wealth in a Proper Manner

Options are a terrific way to put money to work rather than letting it sit about. As a result, the economy benefits from an infusion of capital that would otherwise remain idle. Capital injections into the economy increase wealth distribution and combat economic ills such as unemployment.

The Main Objective of Education

Options trading entails several steps. Even those who claim to be experts in the field of options trading might be fooled. Consequently, the value of education cannot be emphasized. Many traders get the hang of things and start buying and selling options contracts, overlooking the need to first educate themselves. Options exchanges provide many services and information to help traders make informed decisions. Traders who have more power boost their trading activities.

2.4 Leverage's Drawbacks in Options Trading

We will not bother you with lengthy discussions of the drawbacks of options trading. Instead, consider the following list of reasons why traders could prefer to avoid prospective options trading opportunities:

- Options are investments with a short time horizon. Yes, you may pick and select alternatives depending on expiry dates, but you'll always be bound by a deadline by which you must decide whether to act or not.

- Successful options trading necessitates your time and attention. You risk missing out on possible profit-generating possibilities that come from purchasing or selling your call or put option at the proper, most lucrative moment if you don't have it.

- There is no paper trace for the options. For example, when it comes to stocks and bonds, you'll get a piece of paper that certifies your investment.

- Options are "book-entry" investments, which means you don't get a formal certificate proving your claim to or ownership of an option.

- You work in the stock market, a highly volatile environment where things change quickly and drastically. You'll need to be on high alert all of the time, or at the very least find a broker who will.

- Before you can trade effectively, you'll need to be in a rather secure financial state. Creating and regularly increasing to a "trading fund" before you begin your options trading pursuits would help alleviate an unpredictable financial condition.

2.5 In Options Trading, How Much Leverage Do You Need?

There are two more cost aspects to consider:

1. Expenses incurred during the trading procedure.

2. The price of executing the stock options.

Understanding the fundamental cost structure of an option allows you to realize how, even though options give leverage at a lower risk, they still add an element of risk via leverage.

Option pricing is largely dependent on probabilities, which further complicates the situation. Given the kind of price moves the underlying stock has previously seen, you should examine prices considered when valuing an option, but there is one wildcard factor: volatility.

2.6 How to Use Leverage to Trade Smarter?

While investing is a rising pastime for some traders, it is a full-time job for others. Regardless of your particular trading position, you must join the options trading arena with the awareness that you will be one of the thousands of traders looking to make a significant profit from options trading. To put it another way, such people and businesses are your competition. They're driven people like you who get up every day intending to produce a significant profit, with the expectation of making rapid, informed choices, and the awareness that they must take calculated risks.

Gathering like-minded folks in the trading arena to discuss current positions and bounce ideas off of each other is always a good plan. We wholeheartedly support this, and you should consider it as well. But your success is contingent on your ability to make faster, more informed judgments and approach measured risk-taking in a safer, more informed manner than other traders. When you can accomplish this better than other traders, you can find more financial opportunities, make more money, and be more successful. We do not suggest that you ignore everyone you encounter or treat your time trading options as a one-person or one-woman operation. Developing

long-term relationships and friendships with other traders is, of course, ideal. But what we are asking is that you remember that it's your shoulders, and your shoulders alone, that determine your success.

CHAPTER 3

Basic Options Trading Strategies

If you're new to options trading, beginning with a few basic methods is the best way to go. You may go to more intricate methods as you get more expertise and grow more comfortable with trading options.

3.1 Covered Call

A novel approach to calls is to buy a call option with no hidden extras. A buy-write or covered call can also be constructed from scratch. Since it generates income while decreasing the risk of holding a single asset, it has become a popular strategy. The trade-off is that you have to be willing to sell your assets at a certain price, called the short strike price. To implement the strategy, you would first buy the underlying stock and then simultaneously write a call option on the same stock.

Let's say an investor purchases a call option on 100 shares of the company's stock. When an investor buys 100 shares of stock, they must also sell one call option. This strategy is called a covered call because the investor's long stock position protects against losses from the short call should the stock price increase dramatically.

Investors who have a neutral opinion on the stock's future trajectory and a short-term investment horizon may find this strategy appealing. Either to make a profit from the sale of the call premium or to protect against a possible drop in the value of the underlying stock is a possible motivation.

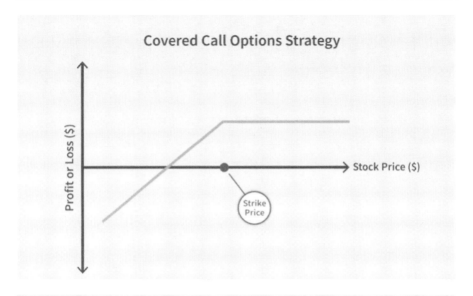

Covered Call Options Strategy

3.2 Married Put

When employing the married put options strategy, an investor will purchase both the underlying asset (stock, for example) and an equal number of put options. A put option gives the buyer the right to sell 100 shares of stock at the strike price if the option is exercised.

This strategy can help shareholders mitigate the potential downside of their stock holdings. This strategy acts like an insurance policy by guaranteeing a minimum stock price in the event of a sharp decline.

Supposing a trader purchases 100 shares of stock and one put option, they would have a total investment of $1,000. As a result, they will not suffer financial harm if the stock price drops. Conversely, the investor will share in any gains if the stock price increases. The only potential drawback is that if the stock's value doesn't drop, the investor will lose the put option's premium.

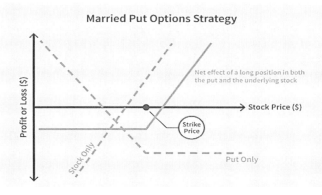

Married Put Options Strategy

3.3 Bull Call Spread

A bull call spread is a trading strategy in which an investor buys a certain number of calls at a certain strike price and simultaneously sells the same number of calls at a higher strike price. There will be no differences between the two call options other than the expiration date and underlying asset. This strategy of using a vertical spread is common when an investor has a bullish outlook on the underlying asset and expects its price to rise by a small amount. Using this strategy, the investor can limit the trade's potential profit while simultaneously decreasing the net premium paid (compared to buying a naked call option outright).

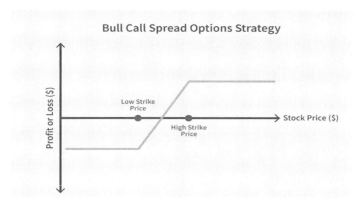

Bull Call Spread Options Strategy

This strategy is bullish as evidenced by the profit and loss chart. The trader can profit from this strategy only if the stock price increases. Profitability is limited when using a bull call spread (even though the amount spent on the premium is reduced). When buying calls outright is expensive, selling calls with a higher strike price against them can help reduce the premium. Using these steps, one can construct a bull call spread.

3.4 Bear Put Spread

Bear put spreads are another variation of vertical spreads. Using this strategy, the investor purchases put options at a higher strike price and simultaneously sells put options at a lower strike price. They both have the same underlying asset and expiration date, and both were purchased as options. Traders use this strategy when they are bearish on the underlying asset and anticipate a price decline. The method carries a negligible chance of either losing or gaining money.

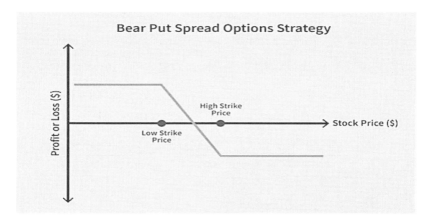

This is a bearish strategy, as evidenced by the above profit and loss chart. Successful completion of this strategy requires a drop in stock price. Using a bear put spread limits your potential profit but lowers your premium. If the cost of purchasing puts outright is prohibitive, you may be able to recoup some of your investment by selling puts with a lower strike price. This is how a bear put spread is constructed.

3.5 Protective Collar

If you have the asset already, you can use a protective collar strategy by purchasing an OTM put option and writing an OTM call option at the same time (with the same expiry). This strategy is frequently used by investors after holding a position in a stock for a long time and seeing substantial gains. The long put provides investors with downside protection by locking in a potential selling price. They risk losing out on potential profits, however, if they are forced to sell shares at a premium.

A long position in IBM shares at $100 per share on January 1 is an example of this strategy in action. By selling one IBM March 105 call and buying one IBM March 95 put, the buyer can set up a protective collar. Thus, a safety collar would be manufactured. Up until the option's expiration date, the investor is protected from a decline in value below $95. This trade-off could force IBM to sell its shares at $105, should the stock price rise to that level before the option expires.

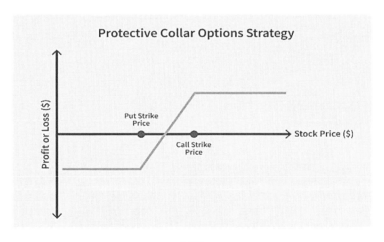

3.6 Butterfly Spread With Long Call

All of the methods above required the use of two separate contracts or roles. In a long butterfly spread, an investor uses call options to combine a bull spread with a bear spread strategy. They'll use a range of three different strike prices. Each option has the same underlying asset and expiration date.

Purchase one in-the-money call option at a lower strike price, sell two in-the-money call options, and purchase one out-of-the-money call option to construct a long butterfly spread. A well-balanced butterfly will have identical wing spans. An "incidental call fly" is one type of expense that can lead to a negative balance. Investors buy a long butterfly call spread when they anticipate little to no movement in the underlying stock before the contract's expiration.

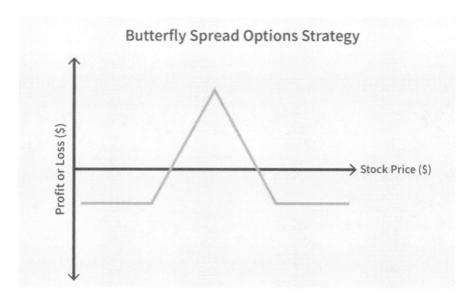

Take a look at the above profit and loss statement and you'll see that the at-the-money (ATM) strike is where you make the most money if the market stays that way until expiration. When this happens, it means that the option is being used. The negative impact on the P&L from the stock's departure from the ATM strikes will increase as the stock price moves farther away from the strikes. If the stock closes below the lower strike price, the investor will lose the most money (or if the stock settles at or above the higher strike call). Gains from this strategy are minimal, but losses are also manageable.

3.7 Iron Condor

When using the iron condor strategy, the investor takes out bets on both the bull put spread and the bear call spread at the same time. Selling one out-of-the-money call and buying another at a higher strike is how a bear call spread is established, while selling one out-of-the-money put and buying another at a lower strike is how a bull put spread is established.

Each option has the same expiration date and underlying resource. Since it is widely believed that this method has a good chance of earning a small premium, it is widely used by traders.

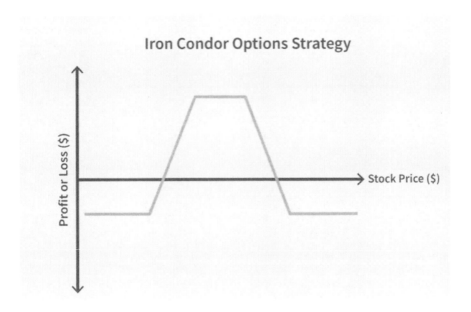

Iron Condor Options Strategy

As a result, the investor might be able to gain from the deal's entire net credit. For larger losses up to the maximum loss, the stock moves further away via the short strikes (lower for the put and higher for the call).

In most cases, the worst possible outcome has more of an impact than the best possible outcome. Given that the framework improves the odds of producing some small benefit at the end, this makes perfect sense.

3.8 Iron Butterfly

In the iron butterfly strategy, an investor will sell an option that is currently at the money and buy a put that is further away from the money. At the same time, they will sell a call that is currently in the money and buy a call that is currently out of the money. Every option is based on the same fundamental asset, and they all have the same date on which they will expire. Although this tactic is quite comparable to the butterfly spread, it makes use of both calls and puts (as opposed to one or the other).

This strategy entails selling a straddle that is at the money and purchasing "wings" as a form of risk management for the transaction. The framework can also be interpreted in the alternative form of two spreads. It is common to practise for the breadth of both spreads to be the same. The long call that is out of the money provides protection against any and all potential losses. The long put that is out of the money protects against the possibility of incurring a financial loss (from the short put strike to zero). As a result of the strike prices of the options that are being utilized, both profit and loss are constrained to fall within a particular region. Investors are drawn to this strategy due to the income it generates as well as the increased possibility of a minuscule gain when applied to a stock that is low in volatility.

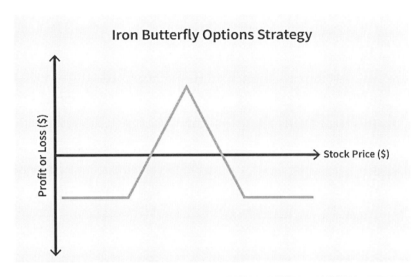

3.9 Long Straddle

When an investor in options purchases a call and a put option on the same underlying resource at the same strike price and expiration date, they are engaging in a long straddle strategy. When an investor senses a shift in the market, he or she may

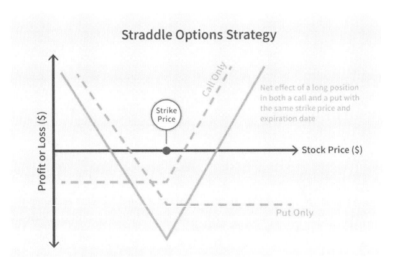

An investor has the potential for infinite gain using this strategy. However, this investor can lose no more than the total price of both options contracts. As you can see in the P&L graph above, there are actually two breakeven points. This strategy pays off when there is a dramatic shift in stock price. The only thing that matters to the investor is that the stock price moves more than the total premium he paid for the arrangement, regardless of the direction the stock moves in.

3.10 Long Strangle

Buying an out-of-the-money call option and an out-of-the-money put option on the same underlying asset with the same expiration date constitutes the long strangle options strategy. A trader who uses this strategy is anticipating a large swing in the price of the underlying asset but is unsure of the direction of that swing.

Bets could be placed using this method in anticipation of positive developments detailed in an earnings report. It is possible to lose no more than the sum total of the two options' prices (the premium paid). It is more cost-effective to purchase an out-of-the-money strangle than an in-the-money straddle.

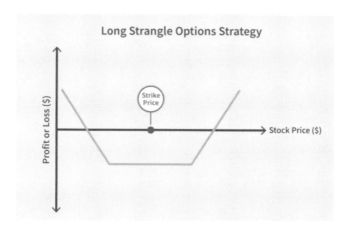

Long Strangle Options Strategy

115

The above P&L graph shows that there are actually two breakeven points. This strategy pays off when there is a dramatic shift in stock price. The investor is unconcerned with the direction of stock price movement so long as the premium paid for the arrangement is recouped.

BOOK 4

OPTIONS TRADING TECHNICAL & FUNDAMENTAL ANALYSIS

CHAPTER 1

Options Trading Analysis

1.1 Combination

In an option strategy known as a combination trade, the investor assumes the role of including both call and put options within the same underlying security at the same time.

What Is Combination?

In the world of options trading, a combination is a word that refers to any options deal that is created using so much just one option type, strike price, or expiry date on the same underlying asset as a single trade. The use of combinations is widespread among traders and investors. A wide range of investment strategies, even though they can be designed, should provide significant risk payoffs tailored to the participant's risk tolerance and preferences for the current financial climate.

1.2 How Does Combination Work?

Combinations are made up of many options contracts that are linked together. Spread trades such as longitudinal variations, calendar, and diagonal spreads are examples of simple combination transactions in the options market. Trades such as the Condor or Butterfly spreads, which are essentially permutations of two vertical spreads, are examples of more complex combination strategies. Some spread trades may not have well-known names, and they may be referred to as a compound spread or a combination trade to refer to them together.

Vertical spreads, for example, are well-known combinations that are often offered to trade as part of a pre-defined grouping. Customized combinations, on the other hand, must be cobbled together with the unique broker and may need the placement of numerous orders to be implemented.

Option combinations may generate risk and reward profiles that either restrict risk or take advantage of certain options features such as volatility and time decay, depending on the individual's requirements. Options conjunction schemes use the several options series available for a particular underlying asset by combining them into a single trade.

In the world of options trading, combinations include a wide variety of broad methods, ranging from relatively basic combinations of two options, such as collars, to more challenging straddle and strangle deals. The iron condor spread, for example, is a more complicated strategy that includes four options of two distinct kinds. These may be used to fine-tune the risk and reward profiles of the underlying asset to benefit from more precise changes in the price of the underlying asset, such as a low-volatility range-bound move.

The biggest downside of these complicated techniques is that they result in higher commission expenses for brokers. It is critical for each trader to appreciate their broker's processing fee to determine whether or not it is favorable to use trading combinations in their portfolio.

Many options big investors and other successful investors use certain combinations regularly because the transactions may be arranged to obtain risk premiums while shielding their money from severe risk.

Individual traders, professional market makers, and institutional investors are likely to have two primary objectives when dealing with a specific underlying asset. One objective is to make predictions of the future movement of the asset's price. The second objective is to keep losses to a certain amount, if feasible. Risk protection occurs at the expense of potential return, either by restricting that value or by increasing the cost of premiums and commissions due to the more available alternatives.

1.3 Example of Combination

In an attempt to include an accurate description, you can look at a widespread combo trade known as a long straddle. Examine the following scenario to see how a straddle trade is implemented:

Consider the fact that shares of IBM are currently selling for $100 each. Due to a major event occurring this month, investors may expect the equity to fluctuate by at least 10% in either direction (for example, an upcoming news event, earnings release, or another similar event). For the purposes of this illustration, let's assume that the bid and ask prices for IBM 100 put and call options are $3 and $2, respectively. Given this data, a savvy investor could enter a straddle trade by purchasing both the $3 IBM 100 put and the $3 IBM 100 call (for a total cost of $6).

As can be seen in the payout diagram for this strategy below, this straddle will be profitable if the stock price moves by more than $6 in either direction by the time the options expire. For instance, an investor stands to lose a maximum of $6 if the price of $100 persists. The trader will once again turn a profit once the price of IBM's exchange platforms rises above $106 or $94. The investor stands to gain $4 ($10 from selling the option minus $3 from purchasing the call minus $3 from purchasing the put) if the price moves as expected, up or down by 10%, to either $90 or $110.

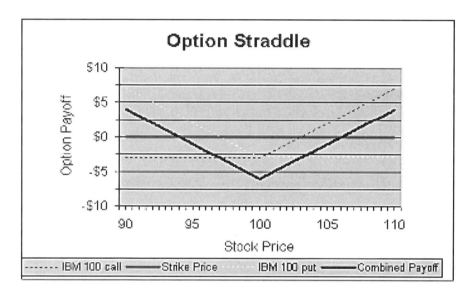

1.4 Spread

To attain specific goals, options spreads are option trading techniques that use combinations of purchase call and put options with the same or multiple strike prices and expiry dates.

What Is Spread?

In financial markets, spread options are a form of option whose value is derived by the difference (or spread) between most of the markets of two or more underlying assets. Aside from the fact that they are based on a unique underlying asset, these spread options behave the same way as any other form of vanilla option.

1.5 How Does Spread Work?

Options on shares, bonds, and currencies are all examples of financial items on which spreads may be issued, among others. However, although certain kinds of spread options are traded on prominent exchanges, most of them are traded over-the-counter (OTC).

The asset classes in the instances above are all various types of commodities. Spread options, on the other hand, may indeed represent the differential in prices of the very same resource traded at two distinct places (location spreads) or between various grades (grade spreads) (quality spreads).

Some commodity spreads, such as the difference between the inputs and outputs, allow traders to get exposure to the commodity's manufacturing process, especially the divergence between inputs and outputs. The crack, crush, and spark spreads are the most well-known illustrations of these operating spreads, used to evaluate earnings in the oil, soybean, and power industries, among other sectors.

Similarly, the spread may be defined as the difference in the prices of the same item at two separate times in time.

1.6 Example of Spread

When traders anticipate that the crack spread will widen, they believe that the mortgage originations will widen due to low crude oil prices and high demand for refined goods. Instead of purchasing refined goods and selling crude oil, the trader may purchase a call option on the crack range.

The link between relatively near wheat futures and subsequent wheat futures, according to one trader, is now trading well over its historical range. This might be due to fluctuations in the cost of transportation, weather patterns, or fluctuations in supply or demand. Alternatively, they may purchase a putting spread option to achieve the same result at a far lower initial cost.

1.7 Volatility

Volatility is a highly crucial metric considered throughout the judgment call approach of options trading. Although it exhibits mean-reverting behavior, the volatility index may be quite volatile at times. This phenomenon is characterized by considerable spikes in the number of black swan events that may multiply the mean number of occurrences.

However, three forms of volatility are the most often utilized in the stance process. These include historical volatility, implied volatility, and future-realized volatility.

Historical Volatility

The option's value will increase if the historical volatility percentage is greater than the current volatility percentage. The historical volatility of a market is often measured every year. As a result of the fact that prices are constantly fluctuating, the historical volatility of options held over relatively short periods may be assessed daily. For investors, the length of time is a critical consideration. For example, the time until the option's expiry date is one of the elements that might influence the cost of a volatility option. In addition, the value of the asset return and volatility impact the price of the option.

Implied Volatility

Volatility is a type of factor that influences the option price and is one of the elements that determines the price. Volatility may be defined as a statistical assessment of the degree to which the price of a market or investment fluctuates over time. It is impossible to predict this component when purchasing a financial instrument since it is unpredictable. Volatility may be classified into two forms in the investment world: historical and implied.

The latter is the underlying volatility, which is indicated by the current option price and is measured in percentage points. According to the definition given above, implied volatility is a forecast made by economic actors on the magnitude to which the value of the underlying assets will change over a specified period in the future. The same kind of volatility is quantified in terms of prices in real-time. With algorithms that assess option market expectations, it is possible to compute volatility.

CHAPTER 2

Fundamental Technical Analysis

Even though both fundamental and technical analysis constitutes essential approaches to the markets, they are on opposing ends of the spectrum regarding how you approach the markets. Investors and traders use both to research and estimate future stock price movements. Both have their supporters and detractors, just like any other investment technique or philosophy.

2.1 Fundamental Analysis

Financial analysis is the process of reviewing stocks that attempts to determine their intrinsic worth. From the general economy and industry circumstances to the financial soundness and management of specific organizations, fundamental analysts are interested in various topics. Fundamental analysts scrutinize all aspects of a company's operations, including earnings, costs, assets, and liabilities.

2.2 Technical Analysis

Compared to fundamental research, technical analysis is different in that traders seek to spot opportunities by examining statistical patterns, such as moves in a stock's price and volume. The underlying premise is that all relevant aspects have been included in the price, and as a result, Technical analysts do not make an effort to determine the inherent worth of an asset. Instead, they analyze stock charts to uncover regularities that may be used to predict how a stock will perform going forward.

2.3 Charts

Because we cannot establish what a news item implies until we see how the market responds to it, the charts are more crucial to options traders than any other source of information. Whenever a price change occurs, it is initially reported on the charts, which impacts how we trade it. In stock trading, the most crucial aspect is reading charts, which involves observing price activity, volume action, and the assessment of formations on the charts.

Identifying Patterns

Traders may use charts to spot trends and build long-term reference lines by using them. Prices do not randomly show on charts. Over time, they organize themselves into easily distinguishable shapes like peaks, trend lines, and times of consolidation, among other things. Traders commonly draw lines on charts to represent the following: highs and lows over some time, trading channels support and resistance flags, emblems, cup and handle, and so forth. These characteristics assist traders in selecting methods, but they also assist them in selecting entry and exit positions.

Example: On the chart below, you will see a "channel" (white lines) that creates a favorable environment for "swing trading." Buying Calls when the market is at the highest point of the channel is an example of a practical approach.

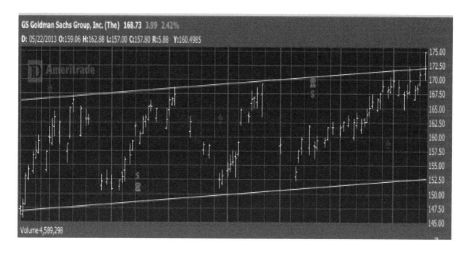

Smart Strategy

Traders may utilize charts to identify trends that might help them make better strategic decisions.

The ideal guideline lets the charts guide you to the most appropriate plan. Bull Put Spreads are beautiful for stocks that have been on an upswing for a lengthy period. The use of Butterfly Spreads or short Straddles might be beneficial to traders who trade in a narrow range of prices. Swing traders may trade a "channel" by using alternative techniques such as Long Puts and Long Calls, similar to long puts and long calls. If a stock "fills the gap," then pick the transaction that best allows for that to happen, then close the deal after the gap has been filled with the stock in question. When option premiums on a stock inflate before earnings are developed, trading strategies allow traders to benefit from the "volatility crush" and increase their profits. Once the trading range has been determined, it is possible to make regular revenue by selling puts and calls that are well out of the money.

Profits

Traders may increase their earnings by following the charts. Once tactics have been established, charts may be used to identify areas of optimum profitability. Because 550 indicated significant resistance, this indicator of AAPL suggested a goal of $550 to close a gap in the market. During the first quarter of 2014, the stock increased from $505 to 550, and we could close out our stake successfully. The stock then plummeted as resistance overpowered momentum, and the stock began to decline. The chart provided us with the numbers for our entrance and departure points.

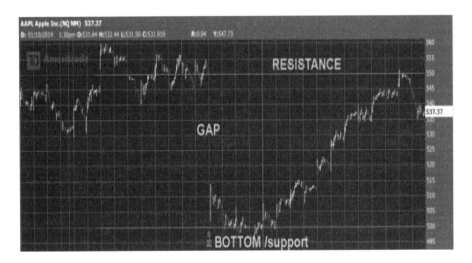

2.4 Options Chain

The options chain may be described as a list of all the available option contracts. It is divided into two sections: the call portion and the put section.

The striking price refers to the money at which the purchaser is willing to purchase the shares if the option is exercised.

Several traders, however, pay close attention to the 'net change,' 'bid,' 'last price,' and 'ask' columns to gauge current market circumstances.

The options matrix is another name for the option chain. Several expert traders can readily predict the direction of market fluctuations using the options matrix.

Additionally, the Option Matrix enables users to evaluate and determine the moments when a low or high amount of liquidity is seen. As a rule, it restricts traders' ability to assess the depth and liquidity of individual strikes.

2.5 Technical Analysis

In general, technical indicators are tools that help traders and investors deduce the most likely future price movement of a financial asset by analyzing past data. The entire discipline of technical analysis is predicated on these signals. This type of research relies on the existence of a regular and observable trend in market behavior. Technical analysis, which involves spotting and reacting to trends in a stock chart, thus provides traders with entry and exit signals that, in most cases, lead to profitable price movements.

Model parameters are something every investor would have access to, but the weight investors give to these indicators varies greatly by approach. Both long-term and short-term investors exist, but the majority of people fall into one of two categories.

The Buy-and-Hold Investor

Buy-and-hold speculators are interested in the long term. They may be putting money aside for their retirement, their children's college funds, or a down payment on a new house. These investors seek growth by purchasing shares in firms that they think will develop in the long run, independent of short-term fluctuations in valuations and market conditions.

The Traders

Mainly in the investment domain, traders inhabit the more dangerous end of the spectrum. In the stock market, they are concerned with producing significant gains by making short-term movements that are profitable. The firm's inherent worth and long-term development potential are not necessarily significant to the trader in this situation. Traders pay close attention to patterns in price movements, and they are mainly concerned with where a stock is trading on the chart and where it is most likely to go in the future.

A number of the most effective of these indicators are as follows:

- **Support:** Support is the price at which a security is expected to bottom out before beginning its ascent back toward the top. This is a major roadblock because it is based on the assumption that the owning market will never agree to let the asset price drop below this level.

  Simply by glancing at the combined data, you can see the extent of public backing for a specific investment. A stock's support level is identified at its lowest point on the price chart.

- **Resistance:** Nothing could be further from the concept of support than this. It's when a stock's price, which has been rising, could potentially reach a ceiling and start falling. This theory holds that stock prices near resistance indicate that the market is overbought. Therefore, it is expected that short-term shifts will be detrimental going forward.

Find the stock's all-time high on its chart to determine where resistance lies. Both the buy-and-hold investor and the day trader can benefit from paying attention to the price's highest point of opposition over the previous 30-90 days, though moving averages may provide a more reliable indicator of resistance. When moving averages are used, the resistance level can be more precisely determined.

- **Moving Average:** Data on stock market prices is volatile, so stock charts will have wavy, up-and-down lines. These fluctuations are typically smoothed out using moving averages. Their purpose is to make the trend line more readable by rounding off the rough spots. To calculate a stock's moving average, traders simply divide the stock's closing price by the period's number of trading days.

The time period over which an evaluation is conducted can be of any length. In practise, however, 30-day, 50-day, 90-day, and 120-day periods are most frequently used for observing the protocol.

- **Exponential Moving Average (EMA):** In many ways, the exponential moving average, often known as the EMA, functions the same way as the primary moving average, but there is one significant distinction. The median value of each day is assigned the same amount of relevance as the closing price of each previous day in a simple moving average. Consequently, the lowest price on average is as meaningful as the most recent price.

The most recent price data is given the highest amount of relevance when calculating exponential moving averages. In contrast, the oldest price data inside the average is given the lowest level of value. Traders believe that the most current data will provide a complete overview when assessing where other prices are expected to go in the immediate future.

- **Relative Strength Index (RSI):** The relative strength index (RSI), a momentum indicator commonly used by traders, provides a measure of the speed and magnitude of price changes in the market. On the stock chart, the indicator appears as an oscillator, depicted by two lines moving in opposite directions as the stock price changes.

  The relative strength index (RSI) is a numerical value from zero to one hundred that indicates whether a stock, index, or other asset is currently overbought or oversold, and is based on the asset's historical performance.

- **Oscillator (Stochastic Oscillator):** Overbought and oversold conditions in the stock market can be detected with the help of the stochastic oscillator, which appears to be another type of oscillator. The rate of change is calculated by comparing the closing price of a security with a predetermined range of prices over a specified time period.

  The stochastic oscillator, like the relative strength index (RSI), is plotted on a scale from 0 to 100. An overbought and overvalued stock, as indicated by a stochastic oscillator reading above 80, is likely to experience high levels of volatility and periodic breakdowns.

- Stocks with a stochastic oscillator value of less than 20 have been oversold and are currently inexpensive, making them a prime buying opportunity.

- If you're looking to invest or make long-term trades, you can benefit from reducing the stochastic oscillator's sensitivity to get a more accurate picture of the progress being made over longer time periods.

- Let's say you want to protect the oscillator from being overly affected by fluctuations in the market. If that happens, you can either take the average of the results or expand the range of trading days covered until it corresponds with the closing price of the securities.

- Traders who are looking to make short-term trades will sometimes increase the oscillator's sharpness so that they can get a clearer picture of price fluctuations in the near future. Technical analysis can be used to make security more responsive by reducing the spread between its opening and closing prices.

- **Pivot Points:** Using technical analysis indicators or computations, a pivot point may be utilized to assess the general trend of the market across a variety of periods. The pivot argument is simply the midpoint of the intraday changed prices, and the closing price from the before the financial day, calculated daily. Trading above the pivot point on the following day reflects the continued bullish mood while dealing below the equilibrium position suggests continued negative emotion.

The Formulas for Pivot Points:

$$P = \frac{\text{High} + \text{Low} + \text{Close}}{3}$$

$$R1 = (P \times 2) - \text{Low}$$

$$R2 = P + (\text{High} - \text{Low})$$

$$S1 = (P \times 2) - \text{High}$$

$$S2 = P - (\text{High} - \text{Low})$$

where:

P = Pivot point

$R1$ = Resistance 1

$R2$ = Resistance 2

$S1$ = Support 1

$S2$ = Support 2

It is important to note that the High price is accurate from the previous business day. The Low price indicates the initial figure from the previous trading day.

How to Calculate Pivot Points

It is possible to connect the pivot point indicator to a chart, and once this is done, the stages will be automatically computed and displayed on the chart. When calculating your pivot points, it is important to keep in mind that day market participants are the ones who use pivot points the most. Pivot points are calculated by using the highest, lowest, and closest prices from the preceding trading day.

For instance, if the trading day starts on Wednesday morning, you should use the high, the closing price, and the cheap price from

Tuesday in order to determine the pivot point positions for the trading day that begins on Wednesday.

After the market has closed for the day or in the early hours of the following trading day, depending on which comes first, find out what the day's high and low prices were, as well as the closure from the most recent preceding trading day.

After adding the maximum, going into the decline, and coming out of the close, divide the total by three.

Draw a line on the chart using the letter P to represent this amount.

Estimate S1, S2, R1, and R2 once P has been determined. The previous trading days' high and low are used in these computations.

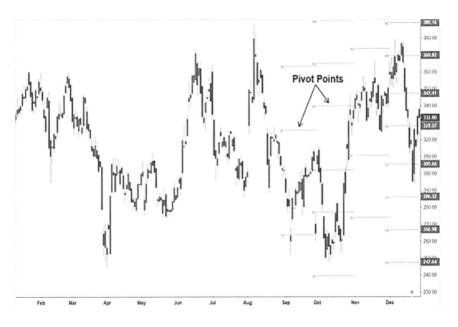

What Information Pivot Point Gives You

Pivot points are being used as an immediate indication in trading futures, commodities, and stocks, among other things. In contrast to technical indicators or oscillators, these indicators are static, meaning that their prices stay constant throughout the day. As a result, traders may utilize the levels to assist them in figuring out their trading platforms in advance of the market opening.

If the price goes underneath the pivot point, to illustrate, speculators know purchase changes. Intended prices for such transactions, while also avoiding levels, may be found at S1, S2, R1, and R2, respectively.

Candlesticks

A candlestick is a unique symbol of a candlestick price movement that allows traders to see the market's movements with a single look. The sector's price is represented by a candlestick that indicates the open, low, high, and closing prices for a certain period. Patterns that emerge on candlestick charts may aid traders in predicting market moves via technical analysis techniques.

Candlesticks are sometimes described as Japanese candlesticks since they were initially used throughout Japan in the 18th century, which is where they got their name from. Their development took place more than a century before the bar chart was introduced into western culture. Candlestick charts are said to have been invented by Munehisa Homma, a Japanese rice broker. They have evolved into valuable tools for traders of various skill levels and experiences. Candlestick charts may be shown over various periods, depending on which is most beneficial to the trader's needs. These candles are available in various lengths, ranging from one minute (in which case a new candle will develop every minute) to one month. A trade entrance will most often be found in the lower time candlesticks for short-term traders when they are seeking a trade opening.

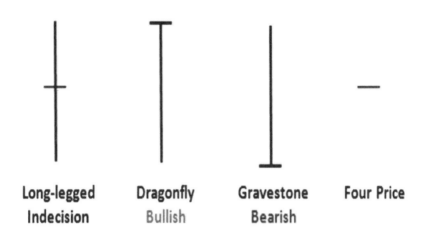

| Long-legged Indecision | Dragonfly Bullish | Gravestone Bearish | Four Price |

Candlesticks Components

Most candlesticks have a red or green corpus by default; nonetheless, on the Nadex interface, these colors may be customized to meet the visual preferences of each trader. In addition to the candlestick's body, it is common to see an above and lower shadow cast by the candle. It contains a distinct piece of information in each section.

Green indicates that the market has risen upward—that the economy is bearish over time represented by the candlestick.

The color red indicates that the market has gone downward—the market is bearish over time, represented by the candlestick.

The top darkness (also known as the flicker) depicts the most outstanding price attained during the period under consideration.

The lower shadowing (also known as the tailed) depicts the lowest price obtained during the time under consideration.

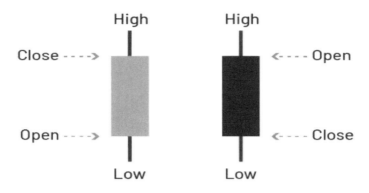

How to Read Candlesticks Chart?

Instructions on how to interpret candlestick charts. By taking a quick look at the various aspects listed previously, you can have at a glance that:

- Which path the stock market has taken recently?

- When the movement was linear, the wick or tail shows that the passage was non-linear; if there is no wick or tail, the movement was linear.

- The minimum and maximum prices reached during the period shown by the candlestick are displayed. It is possible to choose the time frame for your sequential basis, which will assist you in reading and interpreting it most appropriate for your trades. However, although virtually everyone will have a favorite candlestick chart for order execution, most active investors will start the day, week, or trading transaction by staring at lengthier time frames. This is referred to as multi-time analyzing data. It assists traders in identifying a substantial amount of service and demand and the market's general direction. This may be shown by a trader who generally trades using a 5-minute candlestick indicator and watches a one-hour and 15-minute chart to better understand long-term market sentiment.

CHAPTER 3

Technical Analysis of Options Trading

What is the definition of technical analysis? It's essentially chart reading. It is the science (or art) of spotting chart patterns, interpreting them to make buying and selling timing choices, and putting a trading strategy into action. Technical analysis may help you not only make better judgments but also make them more precise, more disciplined, and more successfully manage your money.

Many followers of the technical analysis think that glancing at the charts will reveal all you need to know about an investment.

There are two types of technical analysis:

- **Price patterns:** are visual patterns of what is going on with the security's price.

- **Indicators:** these are mathematical algorithms that take all components of price movement, including volume, and combine them to generate various ratios and analyses that may be used to forecast future price movement.

Price patterns are the patterns of a security's price changes over time. Price activity may be seen in three ways for any length of time:

- Japanese candlesticks

- Bar graphs

Technical analysis analyzes how prices move within a market so that traders may predict future market movements by using patterns from historical charts and indicators. It is a visual representation of a market's current and historical performance, and it allows traders to utilize this information in the form of indicators, patterns, and price action to inform and steer future trends before entering a trade.

3. 1 Technical Analysis Using Charts

Charts are the heart of technical analysis. This is because the only method to determine a market's historical and present performance is to examine its pricing; this is where you begin evaluating a trade's capabilities. Because price activity is the most censorable signal of price effects, it is feasible to show it on a chart.

Charts are useful for determining the general trend, whether it is a downward or upward trend over a short or long period, and for identifying rage-inducing situations. Candlestick charts, line charts, and bar charts are the most well-known forms of technical analysis charts.

When using a bar/candlestick chart, each period will provide the technical analyst with information on the high and low of the period and the price at which it began and ended. Candlestick analysis is preferred because the patterns and related may aid in projecting the price's future direction. Once traders grasp the foundations of charting, they may employ indicators to aid with trend prediction.

3.2 Indicators of Technical Analysis

When technical traders seek opportunities in the market, they employ indicators as much as there are many indicators, price, and volume-based indicators. These are useful for determining the levels of resistance and support, how they are breached or maintained, and how long a trend lasts.

By analyzing a variety of time frames ranging from a second to a month, a trader can examine the price and any other indication. As a result, the trader has a different perspective on the price activity.

Technical analysis' most well-known indicators are:

- Thematchingstrength indexes

- Moving averages

- Movingaveragedivergence and convergence

The last two indicators on the list above are often used to identify market trends, while the equivalent strength index is primarily utilized to determine potential exit and entry locations. Indicators assist traders in doing market research, identifying entry locations, and verifying how transactions have been set up.

3.3 Technical Terms

Relative Strength Index

RSI readings vary from 0 to 100, with more than 70 indicating overbought levels and less than 30 suggesting oversold levels.

Individual stocks, rather than indexes, benefit from RSI because equities exhibit overbought and oversold positions more often than indexes. The ideal choices for short-term trading based on RSI are options on highly liquid, high-beta equities.

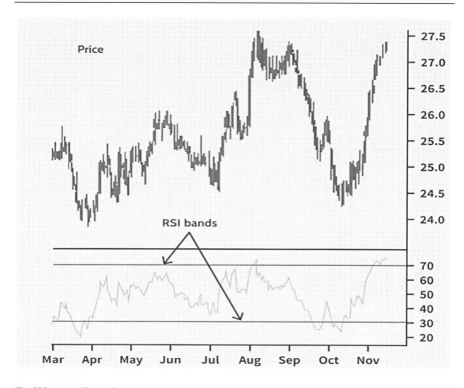

Bollinger Bands

Volatility is important to all options traders, and Bollinger bands are a common approach to gauge volatility. As volatility rises, the bands widen, and as volatility falls, the bands narrow. The security price grows closer to the upper band, the more oversold it is, and the price gets closer to the lower band, the more oversold it is.

A price move outside the bands might indicate that the asset is due for a reversal, and options traders can take advantage of this.

Also, bear in mind that selling options during times of high volatility, when option prices are high, and buying options during periods of low volatility makes sense when options are cheaper.

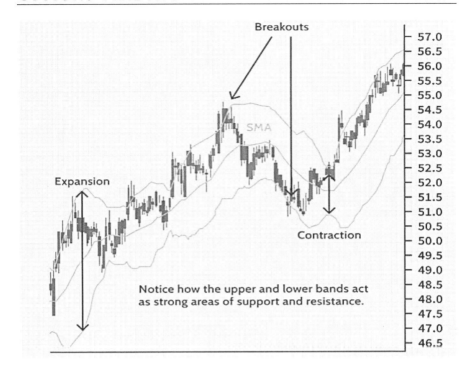

Notice how the upper and lower bands act as strong areas of support and resistance.

Intraday Momentum Index

For high-frequency option traders who want to wager on intraday swings, the IMI is a helpful technical indicator. It combines intraday candlesticks and RSI ideas to provide an appropriate range (similar to RSI) for intraday trading by identifying overbought and oversold levels. An options trader can discover prospective chances to enter a bullish trade in up-trending stock market intraday correction or a bearish trade in a down-trending market at an intraday price spike by using IMI.

To compute the IMI, divide the total number of up days by the total number of up days plus the total number of down days, or ISup (ISup + IS down), and multiply by 100. While the trader can look at any number of days, the most typical time is 14 days. If the result is more than 70, the stock is termed overbought, much as the RSI. The stock is deemed oversold if the resultant figure is less than 30.

Money Flow Index (MFI)

Volume-weighted RSI is another name for it. The MFI indicator is a "trading pressure" indicator that gauges the entry and outflow of money into an asset over a given period (usually 14 days). A rating of more than 80 suggests overbought security, while a reading of less than 20 indicates oversold security.

MFI is more suited to stock-based options trading (rather than index-based) and longer-duration contracts due to its reliance on volume data. The MFI may be a leading signal of a trend shift when it goes in the opposite direction as the stock price.

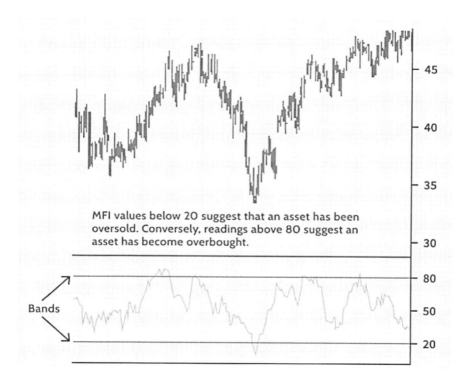

MFI values below 20 suggest that an asset has been oversold. Conversely, readings above 80 suggest an asset has become overbought.

Bands

Indicator of Put-Call Ratio (PCR)

It compares the trading volume in put and call options. Changes in the put-call ratio's value reflect a shift in general market opinion rather than its absolute value.

When the put-to-call ratio is more than one, it indicates bearishness. When call volume exceeds put volume by more than one, the ratio is less than one, suggesting bullishness. On the other hand, traders see the put-call ratio as a contrarian indication.

Open Interests (OI)

The open or unsettled contracts in options are referred to as open interest. The OI may not always suggest a specific uptrend or downtrend, but it provides insight into a trend's strength. Increased open interest signals fresh capital influx and, as a result, the continuation of the current trend, while dropping OI signals a deteriorating trend.

BOOK 5

OPTIONS TRADING ADVANCED STRATEGIES

CHAPTER 1

Advanced Trading Strategies

1.1 Call Options

In the case of call options, the value of the option rises along with the price of the underlying stock. Such options, known as "calls," give the owner the right to purchase shares of stock at a set price by a certain date. This type of choice is the most typical one to see. Call options are appealing because even a modest rise in the stock price can quickly increase their value. Traders looking to make a big profit love them because of this.

What Is a Call Option?

A call option is a type of stock purchase agreement that grants the buyer the right but not the obligation to acquire the underlying security at a predetermined price (the "strike price") within a certain time frame (known as the "expiration" period).

Each contract for the company's stock represents the purchase of one hundred shares. Investors can buy and sell call options without owning the underlying stock.

Rather than buying the underlying stock, visitors who anticipate a rise in the stock's market price should look into buying a call option instead. If you believe the market price will stay put, trade sideways, or drop in the future, you may want to consider selling or "writing" a call option.

You can "exercise" the call option and buy the income share at the higher striking price if the stock market rises to your benefit. In the case of an American option, the holder has the freedom to put the option into action at any time prior to the option's expiration date. No other date than the option's expiration can be used to exercise a European option. Call options trading is another advanced options strategy that can be used.

Understanding Call Option

Let's pretend that a share of stock is the underlying asset. Call contracts are options contracts that grant the holder the right to purchase 100 shares of a company's stock at a specified price (the strike price) until a specified date (the expiration date).

For instance, three months after the contract is created, the holder of a single-call option agreement may have the right to buy one hundred shares of Apple stock for one hundred dollars. There is considerable flexibility for traders in terms of expiration dates and strike prices. When Apple stock rises in value, so does the option contract's value, and vice versa. A call option is a contract that can be held by the buyer until its expiration. This person now has the option of taking delivery of 100 shares of stock or selling the options contract at any time prior to the expiration date at the fair market value of the options contract at the time of sale.

To purchase a call option, you must first pay the premium. It is the monetary value placed on the call option's underlying rights. The buyer loses all money paid if the underlying asset's price is lower than the strike price when the option expires. Maximum potential financial loss is what this expression is referring to.

When an option expires, the premium is deducted from the premium and the profit is the difference between the strike price and the market price of the underlying asset. When this figure is multiplied by the number of shares in which the option buyer has a majority stake, the result is the option buyer's total investment.

If an option contract's strike price is $100, and the buyer pays $2 per share for options, and Apple's stock is trading at $110 at expiration, the buyer would make a profit of $110 minus ($100 +$2), or $8. The option contract strike price is $100, and the cost per share to the buyer is $2 if Apple is trading at $110 on expiration. If the investor purchases 100 shares at $8 per share, their profit is $800; if they invest in 200 shares at $8 per share, their profit is $1,600.

If Apple's stock price drops below $100 before the end of your subscription, it's obvious that you won't be able to use your option to buy shares at that price. The buyer loses $2 per share or $200 per purchase contract, but that's all they lose. The beauty of options is that you only lose your premium if you choose not to participate.

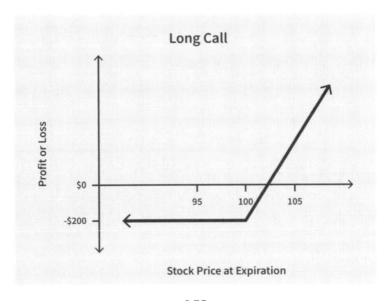

150

1.2 Types of Call Options

Call options come in a variety of forms. There are two sorts of call options detailed in further detail below.

Option for a Long Call

When an investor purchases a long call option, he or she is essentially purchasing a regular call option with the right, but not the obligation, to buy a stock at a future strike price. A long call gives you the opportunity to save money on the purchase of stock in the future by locking in a higher price at the time of the option's purchase.

You can buy a call option on your savings in preparation for a significant event, like a company's earnings call. A long call option offers unlimited upside but only guarantees to return on the initial investment. A buyer of a call option can lose no more than the premiums paid for the option and the premiums paid for the option, even if the underlying stock price of the underlying company drops because of a lack of an earnings beat.

Option for a Short-Call

A short call option's value is the exact opposite of that of a long call option, as the name suggests. By selling a short call option, an investor commits to selling shares at a future date and time at the specified strike price. For the reasons stated above, covered calls and call options where the option seller already owns the underlying minor stock are common applications of short-call options. If the deal doesn't go their way, they can limit their losses by making the call. If the call option were exposed, their losses would be much higher (i.e., if they did not possess the underlying stock for their option). Through the course of trading, the underlying stock appreciated significantly.

1.3 Covered Call

Covered calls refer to an investment transaction in which the seller of the call options also owns the underlying securities. This is done when a long-term investor with a stake in an asset writes (sells) call options on that asset in order to generate income. The cover is provided by the investor's long position in the underlying asset, which guarantees the seller's ability to sell the shares in the event the call option buyer exercises their option.

What Is Covered Call?

Covered calls, also called "covered call options," are a type of option strategy in which the holder of an existing position in the underlying asset (such as stock) simultaneously sells (writes) a call option on that stock. To maximize returns, investors often employ this strategy when they believe the underlying asset will experience only modest price fluctuations.

The premium received from selling a call option represents the primary benefit of the covered call strategy. The premium will increase the return on investment by the same amount that the underlying asset price appreciation boosts the return. In addition, the premium will partially offset the loss if the underlying asset price declines by a small amount.

Given that your profits from a covered call strategy are dependent on the strike price of the call option, you should avoid using it if you expect the value of the underlying asset to rise sharply. However, if the price of the underlying asset drops significantly, the premium received from selling the call will only cover a small portion of the losses.

Understanding Covered Call

Covered call investors should plan for a slight increase or decrease in the stock price of the underlying asset prior to the expiration of the call option they have written. This strategy is utilised frequently by investors who maintain a long position in an asset while also holding a short position through an option in order to profit from the option premium.

As stated, premiums can be earned for an account if the investor intends to hold the underlying stock for a long time but does not expect a significant price gain in the near future. They are also trying to ride out the current stock market slump.

If you own a lot of stock, you can protect your portfolio from sudden price fluctuations by writing a covered call, which also gives you the chance to profit from the premium received for the option. However, the investor would lose any stock gains if the stock price increased above the option's strike price. A minimum of 100 shares at the Option Price must be provided by the purchaser in the event of any intention to exercise the option.

the cost of the strike. Neither the most optimistic nor the most pessimistic market participants benefit from a covered call strategy. Extremely bullish shareholders are better off not writing the option and instead keeping the stock in their portfolios. Even if the stock price increases dramatically, the option's profit limit will reduce the overall profit from the transaction. A more prudent move for a very pessimistic investor might be to sell the stock instead of writing a call option. The reason is, if the stock's value drops, the premium received for writing a call option won't be enough to cover the investor's losses.

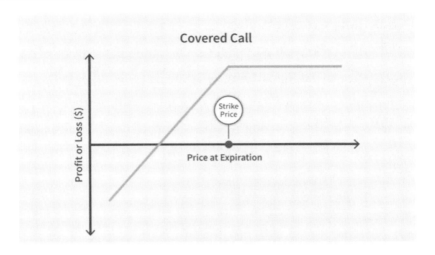

Covered Call

Strike Price

Price at Expiration

Profit or Loss ($)

Examples

Observe this easy example of a covered call strategy. You've made the decision to invest in 100 shares of ABC Corporation at the current market price of $100. You believe that significant volatility in the stock market is unlikely in the near future. You also project that ABC Corporation's stock price will rise to $105 within the next six months.

- If you want to safeguard your income, you should sell a call option contract with a strike price of $105 and an expiration date of six months. Based on the current market price, the premium for this call option is $3 per share in the contract. Future payout amounts will be based on the stock's value in six months. There are three potential outcomes:

First scenario

- **At present, a share of stock costs investors $100.**

   Due to the lack of intrinsic value, the buyer will not exercise the call option (the strike price exceeds the market price). You won't make any money off of this investment because the

154

stock's price won't rise. However, the call premium will pay you $3 per share instead.

Second Scenario

- **There has been a rise in the stock price to $110 per share.**

  If the stock's price rises to $110 within six months, the buyer will exercise the call option. In addition to the $3 call premium per share, you will make $105 per share (the option's strike price). Since entering into this covered call agreement, you have given up a negligible portion of your future earnings.

- **share of your potential earnings in exchange for insurance against loss.**

Third Possible scenario

- **Shares of the stock have fallen to $90 each.**

  The call option will also terminate before its stated end date, as in scenario 1. There will be a $10 loss in value per share of stock, but this will be partially mitigated by the $3 call premium. Because of this, you will lose $7 per share, for a total loss of $360.

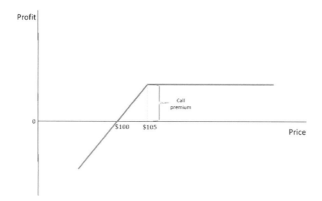

1.4 Credit Spread

A credit spread is a type of options strategy in which the trader simultaneously buys and sells options on the same underlying asset and with the same expiration date and type of option (put or call). There are a few different "strike prices" in use.

What Is Credit Spread?

Credit spread options are specific kinds of options contracts in the financial markets, and they consist of buying one option and selling another option of the same type but with a different strike price. Credit spreads are also known as "credit spreads" in some financial communities. If two options of the same class and expiration are exchanged, the credit risk is effectively transferred from one party to the other. As a result of this situation, the price of the targeted credit may rise, leading to a wider spread and a subsequent drop in that credit's price. Spreads and prices typically trend in opposite directions. A customer will be required to pay an upfront premium in exchange for the potential cash flows that may result from a credit spread shifting from its current level.

Understanding Credit Spread

The buyer of a credit spread option has the potential to generate positive cash flows regardless of the direction in which the credit spread between two specific benchmarks moves, provided that the option's construction allows for this possibility. Traders are able to take both long and short credit positions thanks to the availability of calls and put in the options contracts for credit spreads. Credit spread options are a form of insurance that holders of the debt of a particular company can purchase to protect themselves from the possibility that a negative credit event will take place. The buyer of a call option on a credit spread assumes all or a portion of the risk of default, while the seller of the option takes no such risk.

If there is a substantial widening in the gap between the level of the company's debt and a benchmark level, such as LIBOR, the seller of the option will be entitled to a payment. Options and other factors based on credit spreads are important instruments to have in one's arsenal if one wishes to be able to control the risks that are associated with lower-rated bonds and debt.

Advantages and Disadvantages of Credit Spread

Advantages

- Spreads may significantly reduce your risk if the stock goes severely against you.

- For credit spreads, the margin requirement is much smaller than the margin requirement for uncovered options.

- It is not feasible to lose more money than the amount of money required for the margin that is available in your account when the position is opened. When you trade uncovered options, you risk losing much more than the original margin needed.

- Debit and credit spreads may need less monitoring than other strategies since, once formed, they are often retained until the end of the period specified. On the other hand, spreads should be reviewed regularly to determine whether or not it is still worthwhile to hold them until expiration. For example, if the find a combination makes its way too far and the instantly sufficient, you may be able to open out the spread posture at a net profit before the expiration period.

- Spreads may be used in a variety of ways. Because of the vast variety of strike prices and expiry dates that are normally available, most traders can put up a portfolio of contracts that will enable them to take a bullish or bearish position on a stock of their choosing. Credit spreads are just as volatile as debit spreads and vice versa.

Disadvantages

- The magnitude you spend on the long option leg of the spread will lower the amount of profit you might potentially make.

- To build and attach a credit spread, the incentive fees will be greater than the commissions for a single uninsured position. This is because a spread needs two alternatives.

1.5 Debit Spread

Using a debit spread methodology is achievable when the payments paid for the long leg(s) of the spread are more than just the insurance premiums from the shortest leg(s). This results in monies being debited from the option trader's account when the position is entered. When adopting the debit spread option strategy, the net debit represents the greatest loss incurred.

What Is Debit Spread

As a consequence, a net negative is recorded against the trading account. At that particular moment, the total value of all options sold is less than the total value of all options acquired, and as a result, the trader must put money up to begin the transaction. With a wider debit spread, the initial cash outflow incurred by the trader on the transaction is proportionally greater.

Working Method of Debit Spread

Spread methods in options trading often entail purchasing one option and selling. On the other hand, many forms of spreads have three or more alternatives, but the premise remains the same. A debit spread occurred when the total amount of money earned from all options sold results in a lower monetary value than the total amount of options bought. This is referred to as a net debit to the account, thus the name.

In the case of credit spreads, the inverse is true. In this case, the total value of all options sold exceeds all options acquired, resulting in a net credit to the customer's account. In a way, the market rewards you for putting your money into the deal.

Example

Consider the following scenario: a trader purchases a call option for $2.65. The trader also sells a call option with a higher strike price of $2.50 at the same time on the same underlying securities. A bull call spread is what this is referred to as. With a debit of $0.15, the spread trade has a net cost of $15 ($0.15 * 100), which is the cost of starting the spread trade. However, even though there is an initial expenditure on the transaction, the trader expects that the underlying security's price will climb moderately, making the acquired option more valuable in the long run. When the security terminates at or above the strike price of the option sold, this is considered the best-case scenario. This allows the trader to make the greatest amount of profit while also reducing risk to the greatest extent feasible. Another strategy, called as a bear put spread, buys the more costly option while releasing the less expensive option (the put with a lower strike price). Again, the account has a net debit to initiate the deal. Credit spreads, such as bear call spreads and bull put spreads, are used in the stock market.

1.6 Iron Condor

In options trading, an iron condor is a spatially fair and balanced, particular risk methodology that gains from a stock moving in a range until expiry. It gains from the passage of time and any reductions in implied volatility.

What Is Iron Condor?

Trading in a range between the time the options contract expires and the time the underlying trades outside of that range is advantageous for an iron condor strategy. All expiration dates for the short vertical put spread and the short vertical call spread in a given transaction must be the same.

The iron condor is a risk-controlling strategy that combines a short strangle with long options purchased further out-of-the-money (OTM). This strategy, which is similar to the strangle in that it allows investors to gain exposure to a company without having to take a directional position, is especially useful as time goes on and implied volatility decreases (IV). It's also a way to lessen the market's jitters as a company gets closer to reporting its quarterly earnings.

How Does Iron Condor Work?

The iron condor is a form of restraint that works similarly to the classic stranglehold. A short strangle is a neutral trading strategy that profits as long as the stock price is between the two short strikes, regardless of whether or not the risk premium declines over time.

In this strategy, the investor sells both a bullish (short put spread) and a bearish (short call spread) spread in the same direction, hoping to profit if the stock price ends up somewhere in the middle of the two spreads' strike prices by the time the options expire.

Spread trading positions allow participants to assess risk and potential reward before committing to a trade.

- The initial profit is capped by the credit received for closing the position early.

- The maximum loss (if spread widths are different), less credit received, and the depth of the smallest spread are all determined by the width of the greatest spread.

- We are betting that the underlying will not advance beyond either spread by the time our contracts expire worthless, despite the fact that we will receive an upfront credit for doing so.

There are four distinct types of strikes that an iron condor can use to be classified as a specific risk squeeze:

Get yourself one out-of-the-money put at a strike price not too far from where the stock is trading today.

Invest in a single out-of-the-money put whose strike price is lower than the shot put's strike price.

One call option with a strike price above the current price should be sold as an out-of-the-money option.

Invest in an out-of-the-money call whose strike price is higher than the short call's strike price.

Example

In order to learn the ins and outs of the iron condor strategy, examples are a great resource for beginners. Take the iron condor as an example.

Considerthefollowingscenario

There are 60 days left before the stock expires, and the price is $500.00. There's a gap of $50.00 between the put and call spreads.

In order to assume the iron condor position, you must first do the following:

Make $8.00 by selling the 550 call option.

The 600 call option is available for $2.00.

Do this: o Put the 450-point option on the market for $9.

Invest $3.00 to buy a put option worth $400.

The option premium of $17.00 was collected from the buyer after selling the 450 puts and the 550 calls. It's true that the total premium for buying 600 calls and 400 puts is $5, but that amount includes both options. You will receive a net premium of $2.00 because you will receive $7.00 for the short options and will pay $5.00 for the long options.

The net profit was realized because the option premium generated by the short options was higher than that of the long options. Because of this, you now have a net credit of $12.00. Close to $16.95 less than $17.00. If all of your options expire out of the money, the iron condor will be worthless at expiration, and you'll make the most money. The best chance of making money is if and when the stock price drops to between $450.00 and $550.00, which is a drop of about 10% from the starting price. The maximum possible gain is thousand two hundred dollars. If the value of an iron condor is zero dollars, then multiplying the $12.00 net credit you will receive upon selling it by 100 will give you $1,200.00.

If this deal goes bad, I stand to lose no more than $3,800.00. Multiply the $12.00 net credit by 100 times the maximum spread width of a sold iron condor ($50.00; the put and call spreads are the same width). This yields $3,800.00. In 60 days (20% stock price movement), the maximum loss will occur if the price is either below $400.00 or above $600.00 at expiration. At a price of $438, this trade will be profitable. Taking the credit for the iron condor position ($11.38) and subtracting the cost of the put option ($450) yields a profit of $438.62. At expiration, the short $450.00 put will be worth $12 while the other components of the iron condor will have no value. Resulting in a $12.00 trade, which is the same amount for which you sold the iron condor when entering the trade. $562.00 is the higher of the two breakeven prices for this iron condor ($550.00 short call strike plus $12.00 iron condor credit equals $562.00). As with the lower breakeven point, the $550.00 call option will have $12.00 of intrinsic value at expiration while the corresponding $550.00 put option will expire worthless.

CHAPTER 2

Day Trading and Swing Trading

2.1 Day Trading Strategy

Day trading, in which positions are opened and closed within the same trading day, is a short-term trading strategy. There has been a rise in interest in the concept of day trading in the UK in recent years.

Technology has played a significant role in this development; with the advent of high-speed broadband and mobile internet, investors now have ready access to a wealth of data on the markets as they unfold in real-time. As a result, an increasing number of people are trying to make money off of the ups and downs in market prices by engaging in "day trading," or making trades repeatedly throughout the trading day.

How Does Day Trading Work?

Trading on the stock market for a day is a method of profiting from short-term price swings by actively buying and selling shares. Day traders look for market volatility to make money. There are no opportunities in the absence of short-term price movement (volatility). The greater the movement of a stock, the greater the potential profit or loss a trader might earn in a single transaction. As a result, traders must master superior risk management techniques to limit losses to a minimum while allowing wins to run wild.

Day traders may be considered managers who handle their own risk. While we put our wealth at risk to attempt to generate more money, we will have difficulty consistently producing money if we do not properly control our risk exposure. Trading strategies that work well for us generally include predefined entry and exit points before joining the transaction. Taking emotion out of the transaction allows the trader to avoid over-managing their position, which enables them to make better decisions (proven to have a negative impact in the long run).

How to Start Day Trading?

Listed below is a compilation of day trading suggestions that you may appreciate beneficial. One of the most common types of day trading is purchasing and selling financial products numerous times on the same day. When properly used, these ideas may assist you in improving your trading abilities.

- **Know the Markets:** In this tip, we are not talking about typical trading processes (though it is necessary to be familiar with and understand them), but rather about daily key events. According to what you are undoubtedly already aware, significant news and announcements have the power to affect the markets. Stocks and national currencies are especially susceptible to price changes triggered by breaking news. Maintain your awareness that, even when trading on shorter time frames, fundamental issues may still have an impact on the result of your transactions.

- **Allocate funding to various projects:** The amount of money you designate for every transaction should be meticulously planned before entering the market. You are not expected to invest a specific sum of money, nor should you use up all of your available credit. Instead, you might try investing the amount of 3–5% of your overall balance, which is not too large. As an outcome, you will be protected from the unpleasant repercussions of a losing streak, which will occur for all traders at some point in the future.

- **Make time for yourself:** A time-consuming activity, day trading requires a lot of dedication. In reality, most successful day traders trade for as much time as they would if they were working a normal job. Day traders do not operate on a regular work schedule and instead allocate as much time as possible to watching the market. To make money in day trading, you must put in the time and effort.

- **Make your deals at the right time:** Choosing the most appropriate time to begin your transactions is also critical. The majority of knowledgeable day traders join the market when volatility is high, which is often at the start of the trading range in companies, index values, mutual funds, and consumables, among other things. Things are a little different when it comes to forex trading. Forex is traded daily, five days a week globally—with New York, London, Singapore, and Tokyo being the most famous exchanges—and the biggest volatility is experienced when more than one exchange is open at the same time. On the other hand, certain experts advise beginning traders to trade when volatility is low rather than high to control their risk better. It is your responsibility to choose the ideal time to trade and design your trading strategy following that period.

- **Maintain a sense of realism:** No trading method will succeed in 100% of the circumstances. If the ultimate advantage of the asset you are trading is highly adequate, it may be sufficient to win 60% or even 50% of all trades to remain in the black. It is important to win more games than you lose.

If you remember and use these suggestions in your everyday trading activity, you will notice a significant improvement.

2.2 Different Day Trading Strategies

Following are the different day trading strategies

ABCD Pattern

The ABCD pattern, as the name indicates, is a four-step sequential behavior of a stock that is visible in its charting. Three successive price swings (A, B, and C) are combined with a buy/sell activity to form this pattern (D). This sort of pattern may appear in any market at any moment and over any amount of time. The way it works is as follows:

a. The stock has an early price increase, after which it begins to decline.

b. The stock registers a new intraday low-price level.

c. The stock achieves a fresh level of support on the way up.

d. The stock reaches a breaking point.

The ebbs and lows of a price movement of stock may seem chaotic for rookie workers. Nevertheless, defining the high, low, and support levels gives traders an indication of how the stock will perform in the future. It's an excellent predictor of when to enter or quit a position before the stock begins to rise or fall in value again, respectively.

ABCD patterns are classified into three categories, each of which may be used for both bullish and bearish trajectories: AB=CD, Classic ABCD, and ABCD Extension. Criteria govern each pattern, but the underlying premise is the same for all of them: a variation in the price with demonstrable regularity. An ABCD pattern is distinguished by the period or how fast a stock hits the key levels in the pattern.

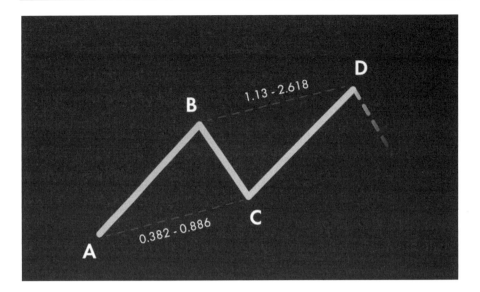

Bull Flag Pattern

During a strong upswing, a bull flag pattern appears on a stock's chart, indicating that the stock is in an uptrend. Flag patterns are so named because they appear on a chart in the shape of an American flag waving on a pole, and since we are now on an upswing, they are referred to as bullish flags.

How to Trade Bull Flag Pattern

Bull flag trading is a reasonably straightforward strategy. The difficult portion of trading this pattern is locating it in real-time, but our scanners, available to Warrior Starter and Warrior Pro students daily, make this task much simpler.

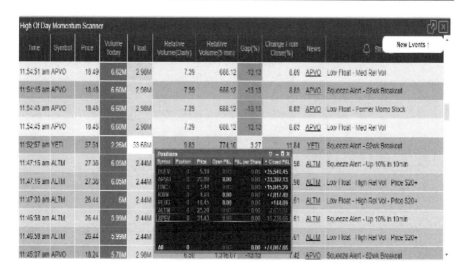

For those searching for free scanners to identify bull flag patterns, Finviz and Chartmill are two options to consider.

If you're interested in trading bull flag patterns, consider the following checklist:

The stock price has been rising rapidly on a large amount of relative volume, most likely as a result of positive news catalysts.

A distinct retreat pattern forms as price action consolidates near or at all-time highs.

If the volume is high, and prices are breaking out of a consolidation pattern, you should consider making a purchase.

It is suggested that a stop order be set below the consolidation pattern's bottom.

The ratio of risk to potential gain in financial goals needs to be at least 2 to 1. Therefore, the first PT is 50 cents from the entry price if you are willing to risk 25 cents.

If you're looking for anything specific in this layout, make it volume. The greater the volatility, the more likely it is that a breakout will be realized.

An additional indicator of a soon-to-occur market breakout is a descending trend line. This section of the flag will be displayed at the hoist. The trend line is very clear and distinct in the bullish flag pattern shown above, which means that the price moved very quickly in the opposite direction after the pattern broke. The line also neatly connects to the other rejected advances further up the line (3 points of contact, including the high of the flag pole).

If traded correctly, bull flag patterns can provide a significant statistical advantage; however, knowing when to get out of a losing trade is crucial. Pinpoint on the graph the instant comprehension sets in that the status quo is no longer productive and a change in direction is required for more precise definitions.

There are a number of potential ways to handle this transaction. The most common location for a stop is just below the consolidation zone. In the image above, you can see where the flag design has been cut off at the bottom. Now is the time to make sure the arrangement is no longer workable and decide whether to continue it or to cut your losses and move on. Use the 20-day moving average as a stop-loss if you prefer.

trading level Consequently, you would have to sell your stock if the price ended the day below that moving average.

2.3 Advantages and Disadvantages

Day trading, like any other investment method, has both benefits and drawbacks. Investors should weigh the benefits and drawbacks of day trading before deciding whether or not to enter the profession.

Advantages

Overnight maintenance of a transaction carries no inherent risks. Day traders don't have to worry about overnight news events that may cause demand to open significantly lower or higher the following trading day if they leave a losing position open.

The result is faster compounding of investment returns (assuming your day trading is profitable). Use the money you made trading the day before to fund a larger position the following day, increasing your potential gain.

Disadvantages

Those midnight occurrences that trigger price disparities forwards or backward the next trading day may be quite rewarding for traders who have positions open the preceding trading day. Day traders, on the other hand, would never have such advantages. Trading more often results in increased trading expenses, which are shown as commissions and fees. Paying all of those additional charges may have a major impact on your performance.

2.4 Swing Trading

In the stock market (or any financial instrument), swing trading is a method in which the trader aims to achieve short- to medium-term profits for a specific time in stock (or any financial instrument). Swing traders rely on technical analysis to identify trading opportunities in the first place. They may use fundamental research for price movements with patterns to make decisions about their trades.

Understanding Swing Trading

When engaging in swing trading, it is common to practice holding a position, whether long or short, for the entirety of a single trading session, but generally for no longer than a few weeks or a couple of months at a time. This can change contingent on how the market is performing at the time. The phrase "generic time frame" is used because some transactions could last for more than a few months, but the trader could still consider them to be swing trades. Because of this, people often use the word. There is also the possibility that swing transactions will take place during the course of a trading session; however, this is an extremely rare occurrence that takes place only when the market is extremely unpredictable, such as the case with the stock market. Swing trading's primary purpose is to generate profits by capitalizing on only a portion of an asset's prospective price movement in order to achieve long-term financial goals. While there are investors who seek out securities that are highly unpredictable and exhibit a great deal of price fluctuation, there are also investors who prefer equities that demonstrate a price movement that is more consistent. A swing trader's job is to anticipate the direction in which the price of an asset will move in the near future, open a position in anticipation of that move, and then profit from the move, if it actually takes place. If you want to become a swing trader, you need to be able to make accurate price predictions.

Successful swing traders are only concerned with locking in a fraction of the anticipated price movement before moving on to the next trading opportunity.

2.5 Advantages and Disadvantages

Several swing traders evaluate bets based on their vulnerability potential. Using the asset chart, they can calculate where they will enter, put a stop loss, and then predict where they will be able to exit with a profit. If they risk $1 a share on a position with a reasonable chance of producing a $3 gain, they take a favorable contingency relation. On the other side, investing $1 to earn $0.75 isn't nearly as advantageous.

In the short-term nature of swing trades, mathematical analysis is the primary tool used by swing traders. Evaluation of alternatives may be utilized to improve the quality of the analysis. A swing trader, for example, who notices a growing setup in stock may wish to double-check that the asset's basis is likewise positive or improving before proceeding.

When looking for chances, swing traders will typically look at recent charts. Still, they will also look at the 1-hour or science and technology charts to discover exact entries, stop loss, and consider taking points.

Pros

- When compared to day trading, it takes less time to trade.

- To optimize short profit potential, it must capture the majority of fluctuations.

Con's

- Transactions in the market are sensitive to market risk during the night and on vacation.

- Market reversals that occur suddenly might result in significant losses.

- Because they focus on short-term market fluctuations rather than sufficiently long patterns, swing traders commonly overlook longer-term movements.

2.6 Comparison Between Swing and Day Trading

The amount of positions that are maintained during swing trading is the primary differentiator between day trading and swing trading. Day traders are required to liquidate their positions before the market closes, whereas swing traders typically keep their positions for at least one full trading day. To put it another way, positions in day trading can only be held for a single day, whereas contracts for swing trading can be held for multiple days over the course of several weeks at a time.

Swing traders put themselves at risk of the unpredictability of overnight risk when they keep positions overnight. This risk can manifest itself in the form of price gaps that go in the opposite direction of the transaction. In contrast to day trades, swing trades are typically carried out with a smaller position size because swing trades are more susceptible to nighttime risk Day traders frequently use larger position amounts, and some experts suggest that their day trading margin should not exceed 25 percent of their total trading capital.

Day dealers and swing traders each have access to a margin or leverage of 50% of their trading capital. This indicates that if a trader is accepted for margin trading, they will only need to put up $25,000 in capital to complete a transaction that is currently worth $50,000.

This is based on the assumption that the trader will be permitted to engage in margin trading.

2.7 Choosing the Right Strategy

Options may be traded individually or in various combinations. Still, it can be difficult to choose which approach is the most appropriate for your requirements with so many trading techniques available. To maximize your chances of success in options trading, you must choose adequate underlying stocks and select pertinent techniques. Some options traders have no trouble predicting the direction of the price movement of a stock; nonetheless, a large number of them still wind up losing out on possible profits or increased profitability because they did not employ the appropriate option. As a result, options traders should dedicate more time and effort to choosing the best options to maximize prospective earnings while minimizing potential losses.

Choosing the Most Appropriate Options

Consider the following scenario: you have completed your study and are now very sure about the direction of a stock price. You have also picked the stocks in which you desire to trade. You're ready, and it's time to select the best solutions to put to use, but you're not sure where to begin. To accomplish their trading objectives or to meet their trading expectations, options traders must choose which option to utilize.

Decide on Your Investing or Trading Goals

To be a successful options trader, the first thing you must do is identify your investing or trading objectives. When it comes to trading or investing, your investment aim is the long-term prognosis for or strategy for your account. It specifies your aims, which aids you in selecting trades or investing activities connected with or fit for the accomplishment of the goals that you have set for yourself. Before deciding on which options to use, ask yourself the following question: What precisely are you hoping to accomplish with options trading?

Are you attempting to predict a bullish or bearish trend? Do you want portfolio protection from a probable decline in your stock holdings? You may be hoping to make a premium income or some additional revenue from your trading activities. Once you have your answers and have clearly defined your investment objectives, you will need to pick investment solutions consistent with your goals and requirements.

You should do whatever makes you feel most comfortable if you're an options trader seeking to figure out your risk-reward profile. If something doesn't feel quite right, don't do it. The decision to proceed with a trading strategy or option type may not be the best one if you will lose significant amounts of sleep over it.

BOOK 6

PSYCHOLOGY OF TRADER

CHAPTER 1

Trader Psychology and the Mental Game

The Psychology of Trading

Trading is fraught with emotion. This explains why you must comprehend the role of psychology in trading. To become a successful worker or trader, you must develop management that allows you to remain calm when trading to avoid overreacting to certain events. This takes a lot of effort and determination. You must gain control of your mind and be able to direct it in the direction of success. This necessitates extensive training.

Emotions in trading can cloud your judgment and impair your ability to make sound decisions. Trading should not be done emotionally, but rather as a trader. You should be able to work your way around them and make them work for you. A clear head and a stable mind should be maintained at all times, whether your profits are increasing or you are on a losing streak. This is not to say that you should disconnect from your emotions as a trader. Below are some of the tips you can apply to improve your trading psychology.

Greed

A trader may be fueled to earn more money by checking their balances in their accounts and seeing it be at a low level. While this may be a motivator to work hard, some traders take it too far, wanting to earn a lot of money right there and then. They make mistakes when negotiating that have the opposite effects to what is desired.

Greed for more money will seek to convince the trader to take risks that are not worth achieving a certain financial threshold in the trading account. These will most likely end up in losses. The risky traders may take risks such as high leverage, that they hope will work in their favor, but at the same time may have them making huge losses.

Fear

Fear can work in both directions, as a limit to an overtrade, or also as a limit to making profits. A trader may close a trade to avert a loss, the action motivated by fear. A trader may also close a trade too early, even when on a winning streak in making gains, in fear that the market will reverse and that there will be losses. In both scenarios, fear is the motivator, working in avoiding failure.

The fear to fail in trading may inhibit a trader from opening up trades, and just watch as the market changes and goes in cycles when doing nothing. The fear of failing in trading is an inhibitor to success. It prevents a trader from executing what could have been a successful trade.

This type of fear in trading psychology will make a trader lose out on his profits to the market when there was an opportunity to do otherwise. It works in a self-harming way in market scenarios. Such traders in this category fear having too much profit and allow losses to run, all the while being aware of their activities and the losses they are going to make.

Trading Psychology Tips

1. Be flexible and do not hold onto the attachment to a trade. If the trade is not right, cut it loose and move on to another one.

2. Changing how you view the market day to day is the key. What you think of the market today may be a completely different story tomorrow.

3. By focusing on what you are doing now you can make quick decisions. Stop thinking you can will your goals to happen just to prove you are correct about something. Listen to the market and forget everything you thought was being told to you by the market.

4. Gain experience and you gain intuition. By observing and experiencing the market, you will be able to gain intuition that can help you make the right choices in the market. Check the chars, and the live trading streams, and maintain a log of the behavior within the market.

5. Use the strategy that is right for the idea. Start with a hypothesis and then build your strategy around that idea. Sometimes choosing the best trade is based on the underlying buy. You may find though that a currency or derivative is a better tactic to play. Seeking out the least risky trade is going to have the greatest potential for reward.

6. Draw a line that you will not cross. Before you purchase a trade find the point at which you can be proven inaccurate. Decide where your market needs to go and then examine what level you will base the idea on to invalidate the claim. This is the location to place the stop.

7. Consistency needs to be executed. Be mechanical as you can be, even if you are doing manual trades. What this means is when I see something that meets my criteria then I will jump on it and purchase it. When trading, you should not leave it up to the discrepancy of the investor's judgment. In order to win you have to toe the line and be confident in pulling triggers when necessary.

8. Embracing the risk and uncertainty of the stock market. You need to be able to see that a trade will be a loss before jumping into the trade position. Expect and accept the worse possible outcome. This will help with the focus along with the trade process.

9. Believing can be seen in the numbers. By following a direct and clear strategy you will see that the numbers will show proof of the effectiveness of the strategy.

10. Individual outcomes from trades should be ignored. Look at the collective of all the trades that you placed, not the 1 or 2 that just took place. Examine those last 20 trades and see where they won and where they lost. The outcome of an individual trade can be masked and will dilute the bias that was encountered by the investor. It can block you from repeating trades from the past that were not beneficial. This will help with future decisions that will be influenced by bias.

The Mindset of the Trader

You want to start a good trade-off with a little bit of humility. Not counting your chickens before they hatch is a good mindset to have. However, you cannot be too negative about a trade, or else, you may jump at the first sign of increase, rather the perfect moment. It is a good idea to be confident in your trading abilities, rather than being confident in the market itself.

It is no secret that it is a good idea to get in the "zone" before you begin a trade. What is the zone? Well, the truth is that it differs from person to person, but the base of it is a mindset that has you focused primarily on the task at hand. You want to be able to psych yourself up for this amount of focus. The best way to do this is to look up some daily affirmations online about day trading. Affirmations are little phrases you say to yourself every day to help you lift your spirits. Choose one and make that your mantra.

Cockiness is your worst enemy. You will pump up your self-esteem too much and start to make mistakes because you feel infallible. You are not infallible. You are human, and humans make mistakes. If you go into a trade thinking that you can't make a mistake, then you are wrong. To avoid being too cocky, you should always remember that the market is volatile and that you are not magical. While you may be capable of making good decisions, you are not perfect, and the market can fluctuate beyond your control.

It is a good idea to have a strong mindset and not veer from that mindset. You should go into each trade thinking that you will not settle for a bad trade. You should have the mindset that you are going to focus and watch each trade like a hawk. You want to be focused and sure of yourself, with just a hint of a realistic approach to your trades.

Thoughts are essential to having a successful trade. You cannot go into a trade with a sour attitude and expect to give your trades your all. You have to leave your problems outside of the market and focus on the trades each day. You need to make sure that you are clearing your mind every day. If you wish to change your state of mind, you have to want to have the right mindset.

CHAPTER 2
Money and Risk Management

Money Management

Money management is a term to refer to the many ways people manage their financial resources. It ranges from budget planning in relation to their income. Money management involves planning and purchasing items that are important to you. Without planning well and a lack of money management skills, the amount a person has will always not be enough for them.

Before beginning the journey of money management, you should be aware of your assets and liabilities. Several examples of cars, homes, retirement, investment and bank accounts are examples of personal assets and properties. Personal liabilities, on the other hand, include loans, debts, and mortgages. To determine your net worth, you must first determine the difference between your assets and liabilities. When your liabilities exceed your assets, you have a lower net worth. You will be able to avoid this if you have excellent money management skills.

Setting goals helps to manage money. Without goal setting, you will be concerned with daily bill management, which will have a negative impact on your long-term goals. Goal setting allows you to see which expenses are necessary and which should be eliminated. When budgeting, you will have to manage multiple accounts. You may, for example, have an emergency fund and savings accounts. You will avoid the temptation to spend the funds on impulse purchases by doing so. The retirement plan and other accounts should be kept separate. There is a variety of software available to help you manage your money. Quicken is an example of money management software; it assists in tracking your various accounts and ensuring your saving and spending goals are on track.

Analyzing, planning, and executing a financial portfolio are all aspects of money management. Investments, taxes, savings, and banking are all part of the financial portfolio. There are economic variables in business management that can affect your company's finances. The ability to access and control all of the factors that may affect your financial position is one of the best money management skills.

You can achieve your objectives by practicing good money management. A dream of owning a home without using student loans and being able to live a debt-free life. Make a better plan to deal with unforeseeable events that can affect your finances, such as job loss or serious illness. You will be able to save money for unexpected events if you use money management.

The internet is a global computer network that contains information and provides communication. Banking, investment, and insurance needs did not exist before. In the past days, customers had restrictions on decisions making in their financial matters, with less information on their options in their local areas. With the lack of internet connection, there was limitation and restrictions on where to find the right information. People had to go shopping for different items, like furniture and electronics. And also the purchasing of mortgages and insurance policies.

Money Management Skills

Do you know your income expenditure? Do you know your shopping, clothing and entertainment expenses?

Money management is a life skill that is not in the school curriculum. Most people learn how to manage money from their parents. Since most people didn't learn about financial skills in school, you can still learn them now. Here are some of the money management skills that you can follow to improve your skills.

Set a Budget

Track how you spend your money. Do you spend on food, movies, entertainment, and clothes? Do you frequently have an overdraw of your bank account? If this is true, then set a budget. Check your bank statements and note down how much your expenditure is categorical. You will find out how much waste of money you are not aware of.

Spend Wisely

Have a shopping list when you go to the grocery store? Do you first check the price of an item before putting the thing in your basket? Use coupons if available. Use online resources and mobile apps to stay focused on your expenditure.

Monitor your spending! By not being attentive to these small tips, you will keep on losing money. It takes time to get coupons, and it takes some effort to find coupons and write a shopping list and check the price of an item before buying. It will all be worth it in the long run.

Balance Your Books

Most people rely on going online to look at their bank balances. By doing this, you won't be able to know how much you are spending at the moment. The best advice is to be accountable by recording all your expenses; you will have avoided overspending.

Set a Plan

You must have a plan for you to accomplish anything. For you to go from location A to B, it won't be possible without a GPS to show the routes. You will end up driving aimlessly going nowhere.

This is similar to not having a financial plan. You will always be broke and not know where your money is spent on. "Where did that money go?" With a great plan, you will be able to track your money and expenditure.

Make a budget and also see a financial adviser to learn how to invest your money. You must ensure that you have the same financial goals and stay focused.

Save Money

Have a strong commitment to saving your money and securing your future. You can improve your financial situation and make it better! But you need to start with the decision to do so. Decide to start saving your money and improving your management skills.

Importance of Money Management

Sticking to a budget and living within your means—is proper money management. Look for great price bargains and avoid bad deals when purchasing. When you start earning more money, understanding how to invest will become an essential way of reaching your goals, like having a down payment for a home. Understanding the importance of excellent money management will help you achieve your plans and future goals. Some of the important aspects of money management are:

Better Financial Security

By being cautious of your expenditures and saving, you will be able to save enough for the future. Saving will give you financial security to deal with any unexpected expenses or emergencies like loss of employment, your car breaking down, or even saving for a holiday. Having savings, you will not have to use a Credit card to settle crises. Conservation is a crucial part of money employment as it helps you build your financial security for a secure future.

Take Advantage of Opportunities

You may encounter opportunities to invest in a business to make more money or an exciting experience like a good deal on a holiday vacation. A friend may inform you of a great investment opportunity or get a great once-in-a-lifetime dream holiday vacation. It can be frustrating not having the money to jump right into these opportunities.

Pay Lower Interest Rates

With excellent money management skills, you can determine your credit score. The highest score means you pay your bills on time and with low-level total debt.

Having a higher credit score, you can save more of what you have and have a lower interest rate for car loans, mortgages, credit cards, and even car insurance. And there is the chance to brag to your friends about your high credit score at parties.

Reduce Stress and Conflict

Paying your bills on time can have a relieving feeling. But on the other hand, being late in paying your bills cause stress and has a negative impact like a shutdown in your gas and water supply. Always being broke before your next paycheck can bring conflict and a significant amount of stress for, a couple. And, as we all know, stress brings health problems, experts say, like hypertension, insomnia, and migraines. Being aware of how you can manage your finances, so you have extra cash and savings can put your mind at ease. You will enjoy a stress-free life.

Risk Management

Risk Management helps reduce losses. In addition, it can help safeguard a dealer's accounts from losing all his or her cash. The danger takes place when the trader suffers a reduction. If it could be handled, the dealer can open himself or herself up to earning money in the marketplace.

It's an essential but often overlooked requirement for successful active trading. In the end, a dealer who has generated considerable profits can lose everything in only a couple of bad trades with no proper risk management plan. So how can you build the best techniques to suppress the dangers of the marketplace?

The term "interest rate risk" refers to the volatility that may accompany changes in interest rates as a result of fundamental factors. These fundamental factors include statements made by the central bank that are related to shifts in financial policy. When it comes to investments in fixed-income instruments like bonds, this threat is the most significant one.

Different from the risk associated with the price fluctuations of commodities like crude oil and corn, which is known as "commodity risk," the risk associated with the price fluctuations of stocks is known as "equity risk."

In the event of a change in the value of one currency relative to another, we are exposed to currency risk, also known as exchange-rate risk. Currency risk threatens the financial security of investors and companies with overseas holdings.

Volatility and Hedging Market Risk

Price volatility adds a new dimension to market risk. Share, commodity, and currency price volatility are measured by their standard deviation. A measure of volatility is its annualized volatility rank, which can be expressed as a percentage of the initial price or as a fixed dollar amount (e.g., $10) or both.

Hedging strategies can help investors mitigate the effects of market risk and volatility. Set options, which protect against a downside movement, are aimed at specific investors, while index choices, which are more general, can be used to hedge a large portfolio of shares.

Contemplate the One-Percent Rule

A good deal of day dealers follows the one percent rule. Essentially, this rule of thumb indicates that you shouldn't place more than 1% of your funds or your own trading accounts into one trade. Therefore, if you have $10,000 in your trading accounts, your position in any particular instrument should not be greater than $100.

This strategy is Typical for traders that have balances of less than $100,000—a few even go as large as 2 percent if they could afford it. Many dealers whose accounts have greater balances might opt to choose a lesser percentage. This is because as the dimensions of your beads increase, so does the position. The very best way to maintain your losses is to maintain the rule under 2 percent—some more and you would be risking a considerable sum of your trading accounts.

Diversify and Hedge

Ensuring you Take Advantage of your trading means not placing your Eggs in 1 basket. If you set all of your money in 1 stock or a single tool, you are setting yourself up for a large reduction. So be sure to diversify your investments—around the market sector in addition to market capitalization and geographical region. Does this assist you to manage your danger, in addition, it opens you up to greater chances.

You may also find a time when you want to hedge your position. Think about a stock position once the outcomes are expected. You might think about taking the contrary position through choices, which may help safeguard your position. When trading action subsides, you may then unwind the Dollar.

Risk Management in Three Steps

1. Before you begin, identify first the maximum money you will place on trading. The money you are willing to risk should not be more than 2% of your bank account.

2. From your entry, compute your maximum risk per share and strategy-stop loss in your chosen currency.

3. To know the total number of shares you can exchange from time to time, divide it by the amount you get in step 1 on the amount you will get in step 2.

CHAPTER 3

Habits of Successful Traders and Tips for Success

Habits of a Successful Trader

Traders who engage in business as a career always seek to improve their skills each day. They possess in-depth knowledge of the market as well as the strategies required to make good cash from the market. So, who is the right person to engage in day trading? Let us look at some of the characteristics one should possess.

- *Market experience* – if you happen to engage in trading without the requisite knowledge of the market, you may lose all your capital. You must be good at reading charts and carrying out technical analyses of prices and market trends. You must also be able to carry out all the due diligence required to ensure you maximize the profits you realize from the trade.

- *Adequate capital* – like any other trade, you need sufficient amounts of money to day trade. You must understand that this should be risk capital that you are ready to lose in case the market does not perform in your favor. Preparing yourself this way will save you the emotional torture associated with the loss of cash in the trade. You must invest a large amount of capital if you want to make more significant returns.

- *A good strategy* – several strategies are involved in day trading. You need these strategies to stay ahead of other traders on the market. Before you start trading, you must understand how to apply these strategies in your transactions. When used correctly, these strategies ensure more consistent returns and fewer losses.

- *Discipline* – it is essential to be disciplined as a trader. Without discipline, it becomes difficult to record any successful transactions. Trading depends on the volatility of stock prices. Traders are often interested in stocks whose price changes a lot in the day. However, if you are not disciplined enough in the way you select your shares, you may end up losing a lot despite the substantial price changes.

- *Patience* – trading involves a certain level of waiting. You need to time when to enter the market and when to exit. Getting into the market blindly always results in a lot of problems. You must be patient enough to get into trades in good time.

- *Discipline*– Discipline is a key trait that every trader requires. The market offers you endless opportunities for trade. Every second of the day, you can trade thousands of different items, but very few of those seconds offer great trading potential. If a strategy offers only five trades a day, and stop losses and goals are automatically set for each trading, then in the course of the day, there are only about five seconds of actual trading. Every other second is an opportunity to mess up those five trades, take up more trades than you should, get distracted or miss trades, leave the trades you're in prematurely or keep trades too long.

- *Have a clear mindset* – engage in exercises that motivate you as a trader. Keep reflecting on the attributes of the stock market and your ability to adjust to these attributes. Learn to appreciate yourself when you win, and to encourage yourself in case of a loss. Wake up early enough to plan your schedules ahead of the trading sessions. Get enough rest to ensure that your head stays clear during each trade.

- *Engage in more practice* – when trading for the first time, you may lack the necessary confidence for the market. As you continue doing it, you may realize that the process is becoming simpler and easier. Your mental capability also increases as you continue trading.

- *Diversify your knowledge* – keep learning about day trading. The more you understand about trading the easier it gets for you when making some important trading decisions. Understand the basic as well as the technical skills required for day trading. This will help you navigate through the risks associated with certain positions.

- *Remain optimistic* – see yourself winning in each trade you start. This will help you set the right strategies. Visualize the market beforehand and motivate yourself to carry out each step required to succeed in the market. You can do this by highlighting the goals for the day and tuning your mind to achieve these goals.

Tips for Success

Understand Your Motive

It is essential to understand what you are about to put yourself through. Understand why you want to venture into trading, is it because you want to make money or because others are doing it? Knowing your primary motive for joining trading will save you from losing money. Trading involves you invest your money into the investment. Therefore, before you invest your money, it's good to learn all that trading entails. Without understanding the market, you are likely to lose money in ways you would have avoided had you first taken some lessons.

Never Stop Learning

For a trader, there's never enough knowledge of the market. The trading patterns keep changing; you need to keep learning why the changes are taking place. You also need to know what to do with the changes and what strategies will work. Learning the basics and understanding the trading market is essential, but a trader has to be more open to learning every time. For successful long-term traders, they have to keep up with new technologies that may affect the market. This means keeping up with the world's happenings as that is what will affect the trade market.

Realize Your Goal

Understand your trading goals, as this will help you push on when the market doesn't seem to be working out well for you. The primary purpose of trading is to get money, but you should have a reason for why you need the money. Having the exact reason in your mind why you need the money will keep you more motivated to be a better trader every day. A clear objective will make you want to keep going even when you feel like giving up.

Identify Your Flaws as Well as Your Strengths

Immediately you start trading. You must identify your weaknesses. The earlier you learn about your shortcomings, the quicker you get to work on them before you are exposed to losing money. You will get to know if the weaknesses are something you could work on by yourself, or if you will need help from other experienced traders. It is good, however, to try working by yourself first since then that means that you get to learn your weaknesses further.

Have a Network of Fellow Traders

Having friends who have been in the trade longer than you will let you know what to expect in the long run. You can get some things to copy from a friend who has been doing this ahead of you. Having friends who are in the same industry will also give you a friend counselor or mentor who will help you in making various trade decisions. You can make this advisor your mentor whom you will consult from time to time.

Love the Trading Market

To love the trading experience means that you enjoy the process more than your love the money that comes along. By doing this, it means that even when you don't get so much money from the process, you will push on with the trade because you love the thrill of trading. The benefits are vital without them; there would be no reason to do trading. However, the benefits will not be very rewarding for someone who does not enjoy the process of getting them.

Stick to What You Know

The trading market is diverse, stick to what you are comfortable with rather than wasting your time going for different strategies. It is good to be open to new methods, but if the ways just spend your time or slow your progress, it is good to stick with what you know.

KeepPracticing

It is good for a trader to first try by practicing to ensure that they are more comfortable in the market before investing their money. Practicing before you finally get to put your money will give you security because you already know what you are about to face. You may achieve this by using a trading simulator, which will help you get a feel of the real work awaiting you.

Don't Be Too Excited

Excitement is good, but in trading, it will cost you a lot. You may be too excited and end up making rushed decisions that will make you lose. Sometimes the market works too much in your favor that you begin to think you are perfect. You may keep getting it right, but you still need to be careful because getting too excited may make you make a small mistake that will bring you down.

Create a Routine

It is essential that as a trader, you have a routine that you follow strictly. A routine will give you the discipline to do things in a more streamlined way. A routine will remind the trader of various things they need to follow each day, and therefore the trader doesn't end up wasting time. A routine will help you meet your objectives as a trader because it will act as a reminder of the tasks you are supposed to accomplish within the day.

Have the Proper Tools for the Trade

This includes having the right tool to conduct your trading. Some traders prefer having a computer while others find using a mobile phone more comfortable. But as a trader, you should have either of the two to be able to trade. A computer or a mobile phone has to be connected to an easily accessible internet as you need to be connected to the market. You also need software that will facilitate your trading. Without one of these, trading is impossible, and therefore, it should be anyone's priority to get the right device before getting into trading.

Have a Strategy

A trader with a plan knows that entering the market without considering the timing is almost useless. A good plan should also include the intended time a trader plans on making an exit. As a trader, do you intend to be in the market for the short or long term? Knowing this will keep you in check on your intended goals so that you do not exit too hastily.

Consistent Research

One way that experienced traders manage to increase their skill level and become expert traders is through consistently engaging in informative research. Experienced traders never assume that they know everything, even if they have been successfully trading stocks for years. They know that patterns are always changing, the market is always evolving, and there is no way that they could ever know everything that there is to know about trading on the stock market.

Keeping a Trade Journal

Keeping a trade journal is a major point of opportunity when it comes to keeping yourself organized and following trends or patterns in the market. Expert traders use trade journals for just about everything, and they keep them for years so that they can reflect on their notes at any given time. In fact, many expert traders even make a point of regularly reflecting back on their notes to see if there was any area they missed that they may be able to improve on in future trades.

Regularly Cashing Out

Cashing out and taking your profits is part of being a trader. Beginners tend to get greedy when they realize that the amount of money they have invested directly corresponds to the amount of money that they can make. By investing more money, they can make more money. While it is important to invest some of your profits back into the investments you are making so that you can profit even more from future trades, it would be naïve of you to invest everything back into future trades. Should you experience a loss at that point, you will lose everything and be back at zero.

Taking Breaks and Having Fun

If you've ever observed a group of professional traders, you'll notice that they're the ones who tend to let loose and have the most fun in social situations. When they are not trading, they are known for thoroughly enjoying themselves and having unlimited amounts of fun. This is because completely letting go, taking breaks, and having serious fun in between trades help to reduce the level of stress that you are experiencing from trades. As a result, you will not be experiencing ongoing residual stress from your trading day, and you will be able to move forward and enter your next trading day more relaxed and ready to focus.

CHAPTER 4

A Project for Success

How to Start Trading

If you are brand new to trading, you are probably curious about how you would sell or purchase security. Any time that the market is open, there are going to be two prices for any security that can be traded. There will be the bid price and the asking price. The bid price is what buying or purchasing traders are offering to pay for that stock right then. The asking price, on the other hand, is the price that traders want to sell that security.

Honestly Assess Yourself to See if You Can Handle It

To be successful at day trading, it will require that you have a combination of traits, knowledge, and skill as well as being able to commit to the lifestyle. Can you handle complicated mathematical analysis, understand behavioral psychology, have an understanding of finances, and can you stomach entrepreneurship? Contrary to popular belief about trading being an easy way to make money, it will require that you:

- Have a never-ending commitment to the day-to-day activities that it requires

- Can take risks

- Can continuously learn without needing guidance

- Have very little leave from work

- Are comfortable with long work hours

Make Sure You Have Enough Capital

Nobody can always consistently generate a profit. Extended and intermittent losses are a regular part of a trader's day. A trader could end up suffering from eight straight losses, and then only recover those losses on the ninth trade.

To make sure that you can handle these risks, a good trader has to have enough capital cushion. When you enter the trading world, and you only have a very small amount of money, you will likely end up failing. Before you decide to quit your day job to trade full-time, you should have around $100,000 that you can afford to trade with. Some novice traders start with smaller amounts, depending on their chosen trading plan, frequency of trades, and other costs they may have to face.

You will quickly notice that the bid price is always going to be a bit lower simply because the buyers want to pay less, and the asking price is always going to be higher because sellers want more for their holdings. The difference between these two values is known as spread.

Picking Out a Broker

During this process, we also need to take some time to discuss picking out a broker. If you have already gotten into other forms of trading in the past, then you can simply work with the same broker that you already have. But, if you are getting into trading and this is the first one you have done before, then you will need to search to find the right broker for you.

There are many different brokers out there, and many of them can assist you with trading. The biggest thing that you will want to look at is the commissions and fees that each broker assesses against you. Since trading times are relatively short and you will enter into and out of trades within a few weeks at most with each trade, you want to make sure that the profits you make aren't eaten up by the commissions to your broker.

There are different methods that the broker can use to come up with their fees. Some will charge a fixed rate for the whole year. This often works well for long-term trades and probably won't be an option available to you since you will do more trades. The two options that you will most likely deal with include a fee for each trade or a fee based on how much profit you earn.

If you can, find a broker who will earn a fee based on your profits. This way, you are not charged a ton if you do a bunch of trades during that time. If you earn a good profit, you will have to pay a bit more because of the percentage. If you earn less on one of your trades, then you won't have to pay the broker as much as you did before.

Before you enter into any trade, make sure that you discuss the fees with your broker. They should be able to outline their fees and can discuss with you where your money will go when you work with them. This can help you to get a good idea of how much you will spend based on how much you earn, how many trades you decide to enter into, and more. Get the commissions and fees in writing, along with any other agreements that you and the broker and their firm agree to in order to protect you.

Tools of Trade

Trading requires that you have a range of tools and resources to effectively do your job—some of the necessary tools that you probably already have. Modern trading is electronic, so traders have internet access to the financial markets. It is a good idea to have a phone if you need to contact your broker, and you'll need a computer or a laptop to access the internet and do business.

Traders need a lot of tools for the active lifestyle of their trade. These include the hardware, software, and other more regular desk pieces.

Computer or Laptop

Technology is constantly changing, so make sure you've got a machine with enough memory and a processor powerful enough that it's not constantly lagging, crashing or stalling (taking to load forever). Most trading and charting software demand fast and up-to-date memory and processors. You can switch between company and broker websites and the screens of your charting software as you analyze a deal. It's expected to have two monitors but not a must.

Charting Software for Trading

Most brokers offer a variety of software options that traders can use to trade and track financial asset price charts. Traders must use trading software that allows them to quickly pull up price charts and display tick charts and timed charts (1 minute, 5 minutes, hourly, etc.).

Real-Time News

That's a moneymaker, right there. Daily, thousands of stock market traders make decisions about whether to buy or sell based on breaking news, so even a split second delay can have a significant impact on their bottom line.

A sudden political development in a major trading region, the release of a government or private sector report on general economic performance, a press release on a company's current earnings, a change in Federal Reserve policy, the announcement of a new product or commercial service, or a natural disaster can all have an immediate impact on the stock market.

Penny stock news reporting services are useful to subscribe to, but their quality and dependability varies widely. In order to stay abreast of the latest market developments, some traders take the proactive step of creating a series of custom searches on a major search engine.

Internet Connection

The internet will be fast enough for web pages to load instantly. If it can't do that, your internet connection may be too inactive for day trading. As asset prices rise, thousands of data points are exchanged each day and stream to your machine every second.

Your internet connection must be able to handle the constant flow of data. You will experience lag if this is not possible (or if your machine is too slow to process the data). Lag occurs when you receive old data rather than new data; essentially, you have a backlog of data and cannot see current rates. Examine the various broadband speeds offered by the internet service provider. Choose one that provides quick website load times and does not cause your trading program to lag.

Brokerage

To be a trader, you must have a broker—a company that facilitates your transactions. Not all brokers are created equal, and some cater to traders more than others. Traders make a lot of trades, which necessitates the use of a broker with low commissions and a trading platform that is suitable for day trading. Brokerage services are provided by major banks, but their fees are typically high, and they do not provide traders with personalized solutions.

Timely Market Data

Trading includes a constant stream of financial data, generated by the price change in the assets and markets that you sell. Your broker can provide market data to you, but you need to ask for the type of data you want. When you want securities to be traded, you need data on the stock market. For example, if you want to see level II data, you must decide whether you want data for the NYSE or NASDAQ stock exchange.

Determine Your Goals for Trading Path

Trading objectives aren't simple, but the principal concepts are straightforward.

The goal of trading is to produce profits in the shortest amount of time from the market action of the underlying financial instrument. Often this is done using margin. Leverage use can magnify the profits from relatively small fluctuations in prices. Leverage cuts both ways; however, as losses can often magnify almost as easily. The first goal of trading is the protection of capital and the production and continuity of strategy and execution.

Make a Successful Trading Plan

A trading strategy is necessary because it will assist you in making sound business decisions and identifying your ideal trade parameters. A good business plan will assist you in avoiding irrational decisions made in the heat of the moment. Smoother trading is one of the advantages of using a trading plan: all of the preparation is done ahead of time, so you can trade according to the pre-set parameters.

More Rational Decisions

You already know when to take profits and when to cut losses, so you can remove emotions from your decision-making process.

Improved Trading Discipline

You can learn why some trades succeed and others fail by sticking to your discipline plan.

Have More Room for Development

Identifying your record-keeping procedure allows you to learn from previous trading errors and improve your judgment.

How to Create a Trading Strategy

Form Your Motivation

Ask yourself why you want to be a trader, and then write down what you hope to achieve from trading.

Determine How Long You Are Willing to Trade For

Determine how long you are willing to commit to trading activities. Can you trade while at work, or do you have to handle business early in the morning or late at night?

You'll need more time if you want to make a lot of trades a day. When you go on assets that grow over a considerable time and plan to use stops, limits, and warnings to control your risk-you cannot need many hours a day.

It is also necessary to spend enough time preparing for trading, including schooling, tactics, and market analysis.

Assess Your Awareness of the Market

The specifics of the business strategy would be influenced by the sector you intend to sell. This is because, for example, a forex trading strategy would be different from a stock trading strategy.

Next, assess your experience when it comes to asset groups and markets, and think about the one you want to trade as soon as possible. Then remember the market's uncertainty and how much you stand to lose or benefit per point of price change as the market opens and closes. If you're not happy with these factors, you may want to choose a different market.

Start a Trading Journal

It has to be backed up by a trading diary for a business plan to work. Use your trading journal to record your business as this can help you find out what's going on and what's not.

You need to include not only technical information, such as the trading entry and exit points but also the reasoning behind your trade decisions and emotions. When you deviate from your strategy, write down why you have done so and what the result has been—the more information your diary holds, the better.

You Have to Understand the Market

A good trader must have a solid fundamental knowledge of how the stock market functions. It's important that you understand the simple details, such as holidays and exchange trading hours, and complex details, such as permitted tradable instruments, margin requirements, and the impact of the news on the market. A good trader should have a wide knowledge base.

Design or Pick a Suitable Trading Strategy

The novice trader that is just entering the trading world should start by picking at least two well-established trade strategies. Both of these strategies will act as a backup for the other just in case one should fail, or if there is a lack of trading opportunities. As a person becomes more experienced, the number of strategies they have will increase.

The world of trading is very dynamic. A trading strategy has the ability to consistently make you money for an indefinite period, but it can also fail at any point. A trader has to keep a close eye on how effective their chosen strategy is and adapt, customize, get rid of, or switch it depending on what comes up.

Switch Your Trading Strategy Into a Bigger Plan

Choosing the best trading strategy isn't enough to ensure trading success. You should consider the following factors to complement your strategy to develop a trading strategy:

- How often you should place trades?

- What assets are you willing to trade?

- How much money will you put into each of your trades?

- How much money are you going to invest?

- How will you employ your trading strategy?

Practice and Comprehend Sound Financial Management

Assume you start with $100,000 in trading capital and you have a fantastic trading strategy that has a 70% success rate. This means that seven out of ten trades will turn a profit for you. How much money can you afford to spend on your first trade? What if your first three trades are unsuccessful? What if your strategy's average track record of seven profitable trades out of ten stops working? Alternatively, if you trade options or futures, how will you allocate your funds to margin money requirements? Money management will assist you in dealing with such issues. Even if you only make four profitable trades out of ten, having an effective money management plan will help you win. You should practice, plan, and organize all of your trades based on a capital allocation and money management plan.

Begin Small, and then You Can Expand

Even if you have plenty of capital and you have a decent amount of experience, don't start big on your first trades using a new strategy. You should try new strategies out with small a small amount of funds and then up the stakes once you see that it is successful. Keep in mind that trading opportunities and markets will stay the same forever, but money, after you have lost it, could be difficult to get back. Start small, test to get your strategy established, and then start trading big.

In the end, the aspiring trader needs to be aware of courses and sites that promise them fool-proof success and endless amounts of profits. A small number of traders only managed to succeed because they invest their effort and time into creating their strategies and sticking to them. There is a big trading world out there, and a trader is completely on their own. Before you quit your day job, make sure that you will continue teaching yourself, stay motivated, design your strategies, and then be accountable for your actions and decisions.

BOOK 7

OPTION TRADING GLOSSARY & FAQ

CHAPTER 1

Glossary

All or nothing (AON): This is a special form of limit order that must be completed completely or not at all.

American Depository Receipt (ADR): A negotiable certificate issued by an American bank representing a specified number of shares of a foreign stock that the bank owns.

American option: An American option allows the holder to exercise it at any moment up to the expiry date. In actuality, American options may only be executed at one specified moment each trading day.

Arbitrage ("arb"): A transaction yields a profit with no risk.

Arbitration: A procedure for resolving disagreements amongst market players.

Asian option: An option whose underlying is the average of a security's prices.

Ask: A market maker's willingness to sell a security at a specific price.

Assignment: The other side of an option holder's position change is an assignment when they exercise their option. The option sellers are randomly assigned options.

At-the-money forward: The strike price is the same as the forward price.

At-the-money: The market rate is the same as the spot price.

Automatic exercise: A clause in an option contract states that if it is in the money by a particular amount at expiry, it will be automatically exercised.

Back months: Other than the first month, there are no expirations.

Back office: A financial institution's department in charge of trade processing, delivery, settlement, and regulatory procedures.

Back spread: When you purchase more options in one strike than you sell in another, you're in a long position.

Backwardation: A word used in commodities markets to describe a futures curve in which longer-dated contracts trade at a lower price than spot.

Basis point: A tenth of a percentile. It's a term that's often used to describe interest rate adjustments.

Basis risk: The risk of owning a cash market position hedged by a futures position.

Basis: The link between a futures contract and the cash market it is based on.

Basket option: An option with a collection (basket) of instruments as the underlying.

Bear: a trader who believes the market is about to fall.

Bermudan option: An option that may be used for a certain number of days before it expires. It's called that since it's halfway between an American and a European choice.

Bid/ask spread: It is the difference in price between the bid and asks.

Bid: A market maker's willingness to acquire security at a certain price.

Binomial model: An option pricing model based on the assumption that the underlying can only move one of two ways in each period.

Black-Scholes-Merton (BSM) model: The concept of no-arbitrage is used to generate a partial differential equation for the value of an option in this option pricing model.

Block trade: A large trade that has been planned ahead of time.

Box: A long conversion in one strike and a short conversion in the other strike makes up an option position. Interest rate risk is mitigated by using this strategy.

Broker: Someone who makes a deal on behalf of another individual.

Brokerage: A brokerage business that employs brokers. A brokerage house or brokerage business is another name for a brokerage house.

Bucket shop: The term "bucket" refers to a brokerage business that internalizes a customer's order rather than executing it on an exchange. Most states in the US make it unlawful to run a business like this.

Bull: a trader who believes the market is going to climb.

Butterfly: An option position with three strikes that are evenly spaced. There would be one choice at the lowest strike, two short options at the middle strike, and one long option at the highest strike. A put butterfly is made up of puts, whereas a call butterfly is made up of calls. It's also known as the spread difference between two spreads.

Calendar spread: An option strategy that involves taking a long position one month and a short one the next. A temporal spread is another term for it.

Call spread: A call option strategy involves taking a long position in one call and a short position in the other.

Call: An option that allows the holder to acquire the underlying at a certain price.

Call-around market: A market structure in which brokers call various market makers to arrange deals. The deals may either be crossed on an exchange or agreed as OTC trades after being agreed.

Carry cost: Expenses incurred while holding a post.

Cash settlement: A cash-settled contract rather than a physical underpinning. Cash is used to settle the majority of index options.

CBOE: Chicago Board Options Exchange

CBOT: Chicago Board of Trade

Charm: Concerning time, the partial derivative of the delta.

Christmas tree: Option positions are a long call and two short calls at two higher strikes.

Clearing: All phases of the trading process that occur between the start of the transaction and the end of the deal.

Clearinghouse: A clearing and settlement financial institution that also serves as a central counterparty.

Close: About the underlying's closing time.

Closing price: The instrument's price at the moment of closure.

Closing trade: A transaction that closes a position that was previously open.

CME: Chicago Mercantile Exchange

Collar: A long stock position with a long out-of-the-money put and a short out-of-the-money call.

Color: Gamma's partial derivative concerning time.

Combination: A location that has many types of options.

Combo: A combination of a long put and a short call option.

COMEX: It is a metal derivative trading branch of the New York Mercantile Exchange.

Commodity Futures Trading Commission (CFTC): It is a federal agency in the United States that oversees futures trading.

Commodity trading advisor (CTA): A company or person compensated to provide futures trading advice and account management.

Commodity: It is a metal derivative trading branch of the New York Mercantile Exchange.

Condor: A long option position in one strike, short positions in two higher strikes, and a long position in a higher strike make up an options strategy. It may be used to make a call condor or a put condor by combining calls and puts.

Contango: Longer-dated contracts trade above the spot price, referred to as a futures curve in commodities markets.

Contingent order: A trade order will only be performed if another deal has already been completed.

Contract month: It is the month in which a contract will expire.

Contract size: If an option contract is executed, it will provide the number of underlying units.

Contract: "derivative contract".

Convergence: As the expiry date approaches, the basis of the future decreases. It may also apply to the shrinking of any financial spread in general.

Conversion: A long stock option with an offsetting short synthetic position consisting of a long put and a short call of the same strike.

Corner: An unlawful activity in which a security's price is manipulated by purchasing a large amount of it.

Coupon: A payment is given to bondholders regularly.

Covered call: We are long the underlying and short an equal amount of calls in this trade.

Credit risk: The possibility that another party may fail to meet its commitments. Counterparty risk is another term for this.

Cross: When a broker has both the buy and sell sides of an order, he may execute it. In most cases, exchanges have procedures that enable other traders to join in on these deals if they want.

Day order: An order that is only valid for one day.

Deck: It's the order book of a broker.

Deep (in-the-money): A long-term option position that is well in the money.

Default: A market participant's failure to satisfy their commitments.

Delivery date: The deadline by which a futures contract seller must satisfy his promises.

Delivery options: The alternatives are open to a futures seller. Timing options, wildcard options, and quality options are all examples of these.

Delivery price: When a futures contract is delivered, the price at which it is settled is called the settlement price.

Delta neutral: A strategy that has a zero delta.

Delta: The option's value's derivative concerning the underlying. By definition, this represents the option's hedge ratio and the trader's exposure to the underlying.

Derivative: A financial instrument whose price may be calculated using the price.

Designated primary market maker (DPM): On the CBOE, a kind of trader who is required to supply a particular level of liquidity. This job is a cross between a market maker and a specialist.

Diagonal spread: A position in which a long option in one month is offset by a short option of the same kind in a different month and strike.

Dispersion trading: A trading technique in which a short position in index options is compensated by a long position in index component options.

Dispersion: A metric that measures the misalignment between an index's volatility and the volatility of its members.

Dividend yield: Dividend yield is the yearly percentage return a stockholder receives through dividends.

Dividend: A cash payment made to the owner of stock regularly.

Dynamic hedge: As the underlying moves, trade in the underlying is made to offset the deltas generated from a gamma position.

Elasticity: The percentage rise in an option's value for a 1% change in the underlying price.

Electronic communication network (ECN): A computer system that enables transactions outside of an exchange.

Electronic exchange: A derivatives exchange that uses computers to handle trade.

Equity: (1) A stock; (2) a trading account's liquidation value.

European-style option: An option that can't be used until it's beyond its expiry date.

Exchange rate: The exchange rate at which one currency may be exchanged for another.

Exchange: A market in which an asset or a derivative is exchanged.

Exchange-traded fund (ETF): Exchange-traded closed-end funds.

Execution: The procedure for executing a trading order for securities.

Exercise price (strike): It is the price at which the buyer of a call or put option may purchase or sell the underlying asset.

Exercise: The right to purchase or sell the underlying security is activated.

Expiration date: The date on which an option may be exercised for the final time.

Expiration: The expiration date of the option's ability to be exercised.

Extrinsic value (time value): An option's price minus its inherent value. Extrinsic (or temporal) value is the only component of out-of-the-money (OTM) options.

Fair market value: The worth of an asset in normal conditions.

Fair Value: The Black-Scholes Options Pricing Model is used to calculate an option's theoretical value.

Fibonacci retracement: When prices on a chart swing 38.2%, 50%, or 61.8% off their prior peaks or bottoms before resuming their original trend direction. 50 % is the most frequent and simplest to see.

Fill or kill: An order that must be satisfied with a certain number of contracts or it will be canceled.

FIll order: An order that must be completed right now or canceled.

Fill: A command that was carried out.

Floor broker: An exchange member who gets compensated for executing orders.

Floor trader: It is an exchange member who trades for his account on the exchange's floor.

Fundamental analysis: An examination of stock security based on its capacity to make a profit for its shareholders. This kind of study includes earnings, PE ratios, EPS, net assets, liabilities, customers, and so on.

Futures contracts: An agreement to purchase or sell an underlying security at a certain price on a set date. The difference between options and futures is that the buyer has the right to purchase rather than the duty to purchase with options. Both groups in a futures contract are obligated to keep their end of the arrangement.

Gamma: The difference between the rate at which delta varies and the rate at which the underlying asset moves.

Gap: When the starting bar of a price chart opens and remains above (lower or higher) the preceding bar's spread. Gaps may be little or large.

Good till canceled: An order that stays open until either filled or explicitly canceled by the trader (GTC).

Guts spread: Buying ITM calls and puts to mirror the risk profile is an expensive approach. It is considerably less expensive to trade a strangle than trade guts.

Hedge: Taking multiple positions through options, futures, or other derivatives to reduce the risk of one stake.

Historic (statistical): A measure of an asset's price variation averages out volatility over time. 21–23 trade days is a common and popular timeframe.

If implied volatility falls, the word may also refer to an investment that will gain value.

Index options: Options based on stock or other security indices.

Index: A collection of assets exchanged as single security (typically in the same industry or market size).

Interest rates: The lender's interest rate on borrowed funds is generally expressed as a percentage.

In-the-money (ITM): Where you may earn by exercising an option. The current stock price is more than the call strike price in ITM calls. The current stock price is less than the put strike price in ITM puts.

Intrinsic Value: The value of an option that is in the money.

Iron Butterfly: A four-leg option strategy that combines calls and puts.

Japanese candlesticks: The open, high, low, and close price bars are indicated in this common manner of graphically showing price bars. Price bars that move upward are hollow. The pricing bars that go downward have been filled. Different-looking price bars and price clusters might lead to various perceptions of future price changes.

LEAPs: Equity Anticipation Securities with a Long Time Horizon. These are long-term stock options that have a three-year expiry date. LEAPs are American-style trading options that come in calls and puts.

Leg in/leg out: Legging into a spread comprises finishing just one part of a spread to complete the other parts later at a lower price. Legging out of a spread is exiting your spread one part at a time to complete the remaining parts at better prices when the underlying asset moves in the expected direction.

Leg: A spread's one side or component.

Limit order: An order to purchase a security at a fixed price equal to or less than the current price of the security. An order to sell at a fixed price equal to or more than the security's current price.

Liquidity: The rate at which an asset may be exchanged and the ease with which it can be traded. Cash is the most liquid asset, but the property (real estate) is one of the least liquid.

Long: You are a buyer of security if you are long.

MACD (Moving Average Convergence Divergence): A momentum indicator measures the difference between two moving averages. Momentum rises when the moving averages move apart and vice versa.

Margin account: It is a brokerage account in which the client borrows a portion of the net debit necessary to execute a deal from the brokerage.

Margin call: When the brokerage contacts the account holder to request that they deposit additional monies into their account to keep the deal open. It's worth noting that techniques that include infinite risk sometimes need a margin amount set by the brokerage.

Margin requirements: The minimum amount of cash or marginable assets (such as blue-chip stocks) required in an account to write uncovered (or naked) options.

Margin: Amount paid by the account holder (in cash or "marginable securities") kept by the brokerage as collateral against noncash or high-risk investments, or if the brokerage has given the account holder the funds to execute a deal.

Mark to market: The process of adjusting margin accounts daily to reflect earnings and losses in such a manner that losses do not build.

Market capitalization: The value per share multiplied by the number of outstanding shares.

Market if touched (MIT) order: If the stated price is attained, the order becomes a market order.

Market maker: A trader or trading business that facilitates trading by buying and selling securities in a market. Market makers create a two-sided (bid and ask) market.

Market on Close order: This is an order that instructs the broker to get the best price at the closing of the trade or during the final five minutes.

Market on open order: An order must be filled at the start of the trading day.

Market order: To ensure execution, trade securities quickly at the best market prices.

Market price: The price of the most recent transaction.

Mid-curve Option: A short-term option on a long-term futures contract in the futures options markets. Mid-curve options are the most frequent in euro-currency futures markets, such as Eurodollars and Euribor.

Momentum: The point at which the market's direction (up or down) is determined.

Naked: A long (short) market position with no short (long) market position to balance it out.

Neutral Spread: A risk-neutral spread in terms of one or more risk measures, the most common of which is the delta. When the total number of long and short contracts of the same kind is equal, a spread is a lot of neutral.

Not Held: An order is submitted to a broker, but the broker controls when and how it is executed.

Omega (Ω): The Greek letter is occasionally used to indicate the flexibility of an option.

One-Cancels-the-Other (OCO): Two orders are filed simultaneously, and anyone may be implemented. When one order is carried out, the other is instantly canceled.

Order Book Official (OBO): A member of the exchange who executes market or limits orders for public consumers.

Out of the Money: A choice with no inherent value at the moment. If the exercise price of a call is more than the current price of the underlying contract, the call is out of money. If the exercise price of a put is less than the current price of the underlying agreement, the put is out of the money. Out of the Money Forward refers to an option with no inherent value compared to the underlying contract's forward price.

Out-Option: If the underlying instrument trades at a preset price before expiry, the option is said to have expired. A knock-out option is also known as a knock-out option.

Out-Price: Before an out-option is declared to have expired, the underlying instrument must trade at a certain price.

Out-Trade: A deal that the clearinghouse cannot complete because the two parties to the trade have supplied contradictory information.

Overwrite: The selling of an option against an existing underlying contract position.

Pin Risk: The risk to the seller of an option that will be precisely in the money upon expiry. The vendor will have no idea whether or not the option will be used.

Portfolio Insurance: The technique of regularly adjusting the number of holdings in an underlying asset to imitate the features of an option on the underlying instrument. It is analogous to the delta-neutral dynamic hedging strategy for capturing the value of a mispriced option.

Position Limit: It is the maximum number of open contracts in the same underlying market that an exchange or clearinghouse will allow for a particular trader or company.

Position: The total number of open contracts in a certain underlying market held by a trader.

Premium: The cost of an option.

Program Trading: The purchase or selling of a commodity as part of an arbitrage plan. An upcoming contract of the stock index against an opposite stake in the index's constituent stocks component.

Put Option: It is a contract between a buyer and a seller in which the buyer gets the right, but not the duty, to sell a defined underlying contract at a predetermined price on or before a certain date. If the buyer chooses to exercise his put option, the seller of the put option is responsible for taking delivery of the underlying contract.

Ratchet Option: The underlying price over a series of defined time intervals during the option's life determines the minimum value of this exotic option.

Ratio Spread: A spread in which the number of long market contracts (long underlying, long call, or short put) is greater than the number of short market contracts (short underlying, short call, or long put).

Ratio Write: Multiple options are sold against an underlying contract's current position.

Reverse Conversion: A synthetic long underlying position and a short underlying position. The synthetic position comprises a long call and a short put option with an identical exercise price and expiration date. Also referred to as a Reversal.

Rho (P): The theoretical sensitivity of an option's theoretical value to interest rate changes.

Risk Reversal: A long (short) underlying position, as well as a long (short) out-of-the-money, put and a short (long) out-of-the-money call both selections must be valid for the same amount of time. A Split-Strike Conversion is also known as a Split-Strike Conversion. The role is comparable to that of a Collar.

Roll: It is a long call and a short put with the same expiry date and a short call and a long put with a separate expiration date. The exercise price of all four options must be the same, and the underlying stock or commodity must be the same.

Scalper: An exchange floor trader who seeks to benefit by purchasing at the bid price and selling at the offer price in a certain market. After each trading day, most scalpers strive to close out all of their holdings.

Serial Option: An future exchange option expiry without a matching futures expiration. A serial option's underlying contract is the next futures contract beyond the option's expiry date.

Series: All options apply to the identical underlying contract, exercise price, and expiry date.

Short Premium: If the underlying contract does not change or moves extremely slowly, this position will potentially gain value. Should the underlying market make a huge or rapid move in either direction, the position's value would potentially drop.

Short Ratio Spread: This is called a spread when more options are sold than bought.

Short Squeeze: A circumstance that arises in the stock options market, frequently due to a partial tender offer in which no shares may be borrowed to maintain a short stock position. If a trader is assigned a short-call position, they may be required to execute the position. Even if the call still has some time left on the clock to satisfy his delivery duties, there is still a time value left.

Short: A position acquired due to the selling of a contract. A position that would potentially grow (drop) in value if the price of the underlying contract falls is sometimes referred to as a call option (rise). A short (long) put position is equivalent to a long (short) market position.

Sigma (σ): The most often used standard deviation notation. Because standard deviation is often used to describe volatility, the same notation is frequently employed to signify volatility.

Specialist: An exchange gives a market maker exclusive rights to establish a market in a certain contract or collection of contracts. A specialist may either purchase or sell for his account or operate as a broker for other people. An expert must ensure that the market is fair and orderly in exchange.

Speculator: A trader hoping to benefit from a certain directional movement in an underlying contract.

Speed: The gamma of an option's sensitivity to a change in the underlying price.

Spread: A long market position and an offsetting short market position in contracts with the same underlying market are common, although not necessarily.

Stock-Type Settlement: A settlement method in which the buyer must pay the seller in full and right away after purchasing a contract. Until the position is liquidated, all gains and losses from the transaction remain unrealized.

Stop (Loss) Order: If the contract trades at a defined price, the contingency order becomes a market order.

Stop-Limit Order: If the contract trades at a certain price, the contingency order becomes a limit order.

Straddle: A long (short) call and a long (short) put are options with the same underlying contract, expiry date, and exercise price.

Strangle: A long (short) call and a long (short) put are two options with the same underlying contract, expiry date, and exercise prices but different exercise prices.

Strap: An old phrase for a position consists of two long (short) calls and one long (short) put, with the same underlying contract, expiry date, and exercise price for all options.

Strip: An old phrase for a position that consists of one long (short) call and two long (short) puts, with the identical underlying contract, expiry date, and exercise price for all options. A series of futures or futures options meant to mirror

Swap: A contract for the exchange of cash flows. A swap is most typically used to convert variable-interest-rate payments to fixed-interest-rate payments.

Swaption: The possibility of entering into a swap deal.

Synthetic Call: A long (short) put with a long (short) underlying position.

Synthetic Put: A long (short) call with a short (long) underlying position.

Synthetic Underlying: A long (short) call and a short (long) put are two options with the same underlying contract, expiry date, and exercise price.

Synthetic: A collection of contracts that, when combined, have the same qualities as another contract.

Tau (τ): The most popular marker for the length of time till expiry. The sensitivity of an option's theoretical value to a change in volatility is also referred to by some traders (equivalent to the vega)

Term Structure: In the same underlying market, implied volatilities are distributed over multiple expiry months.

The characteristics of a long-term interest-rate position, or a series of futures or futures options designed to match the characteristics of a long-term interest-rate position in Eurocurrency markets.

Theoretical Value: A mathematical model generates an option value based on previous assumptions about the option's terms, the underlying contract's features, and current interest rates. Fair value is another name for it.

Three-Way: A long or short position in the underlying instrument has been substituted with a very deeply in-the-money call or put, analogous to a conversion or reversal.

Time value: An option's price minus its inherent value. An out-of-the-money option's pricing is purely determined by time value. Also known as Time Premium or Extrinsic Value.

Timebox: A deeply in-the-money call or put, equivalent to a conversion or reversal, has been replaced for varying positions in the underlying instrument.

Type: A call or a put option may be bought or sold.

Underlying: If an option is exercised, this is the instrument provided.

Vanilla Option: An option, as opposed to an exotic option, that is normally exchange-traded and has standardized and conventional contract parameters.

Vanna: The degree to which an option's delta is affected by changes in volatility.

Variation: The daily cash flow generated by changes in a futures contract's settlement price.

Vertical Spread: The purchase of one option at one exercise price and the selling of another option at a different exercise price, both of which are of the same kind, have the same underlying contract, and expire simultaneously.

Volatility: The extent to which a contract's price tends to change over time.

Warrant: An option for a long-term call. A warrant's expiry date is subject to change. The issuer may extend the term in specific instances.

Write: To provide an option for sale.

Zero-Cost Collar: The price of the acquired and sold options is equal in a collar.

Zomma: The gamma of an option's susceptibility to changes in volatility.

CHAPTER 2

Frequently Asked Questions

What is a dividend, exactly?

A premium is a regularly used term in the business/finance industry in the stock market sector.

Whether you know what the term means or not, a dividend is a piece or fragment of a company's earnings sent to shareholders.

Put another way, the dividend is paid to your company's shareholders. The premium must be paid according to each shareholder's shares, either as an additional incentive to encourage investors to acquire stocks or periodically, depending on the company's procedure, agreement, or arrangement with shareholders.

How can you choose the best firm to invest in?

You may invest in a variety of businesses. Each firm, on the other hand, functions uniquely. If the company's policy or agreement benefits you, the investment will pay off in the long term. However, selecting the correct firm should be a top priority for a novice. Keep the following suggestions in mind for selecting a company:

- Invest in stocks that enable you to have a thorough understanding of the business and structural model of the firm. For example, to invest in Apple or Amazon, you must have a thorough grasp of their operations.

- Invest in firms with a strong structure, strategy, and business model. Renowned and competent organizations with distinctive layouts are all great and recognized brands on Forbes today.

- Check out the company's financial situation. Do they have any legal proceedings pending in court? How many times have they been forced to declare bankruptcy?

- How many stockholders are they known to have? What are the stock market's thoughts on them? Do they constantly create news on topics like fraud, insolvency, or illicit marketing? Focus on firms ready to offer dividends to their investors; each firm has a policy that makes them distinct from others.

What's the difference between stock and FX trading?

Even though both are good financial vehicles, the forex market differs from the stock market. If you're unsure what the difference between forex and stock trading is, here's a quick rundown. Buying and selling currencies are what forex trading entails. It's not the same as purchasing stocks; when you trade stocks, you're either buying or selling shares.

What is a shareholder's role?

We understand that the prospect of profit motivates you to purchase and sell stocks. However, being a shareholder entails much more than simply profit. Nevertheless, it would help if you accepted certain duties. A shareholder's obligations are as follows:

- In the corporation, a shareholder brainstorms and takes choices. A company's board of directors has no authority to make decisions, make changes, dismiss, or replace key management or executive without first telling the shareholders.

- Shareholders determine how much the company's workers, personnel, and directors earn. Shareholders have the authority to amend the company's constitution or policies. Shareholders create, review, and approve a company's financial initiatives and statements.

How do I go about becoming a stockbroker?

You're probably aware that stocks may be purchased and sold, but not everyone who buys and sells supplies is a stockbroker. A middleman, most often a distributor, is constantly present in the commercial sector. A stockbroker is a middleman in the stock market.

What is the stockbroker's role?

A stockbroker is a person who sells and buys stocks. They might work as a consultant, advising clients interested in the stock market, and they also may be hired to keep track of an investor's investments.

Being a stockbroker may be difficult, but it can also be rewarding, and you must understand your alternatives if you

want to succeed. You should be a registered member of the Financial Industry Regulatory Authority in your nation and pass your tests to become a certified broker.

What is the smallest amount required to purchase a stock?

People often ask this question. You may invest any amount of money in stocks. However, only those who begin investing should set aside at least six months' worth of income. So, if your monthly salary is

$1,000 and you save $500 each month, you will have $3000 at the end of six months. That should be enough to purchase some shares and make you a nice profit.

What is the difference between mutual assets and the stock market?

Apart from that, they both produce profits. Mutual funds and the stock market are not the same.

The stock market entails purchasing a company's shares and stocks, becoming a shareholder, and profiting. On the other hand, mutual funds are a kind of collective investment that brings together a variety of participants to purchase bonds, money, or stocks.

When I lose money in the stock market, what happens?

Every company has ups and downs, and trust me when we say the stock market is no exception. You may lose money in the stock market for various reasons, including the stock market collapse, one of the most typical.

A stock market collapse is characterized by a sharp drop in stock values across the board. When deflation occurs, it results in a huge loss of paper wealth. What should you do if this happens? Get your act together, get financial advice, recover from the loss, learn from the experience, and reinvest.

What does it mean to sell a stock short?

Shorting a stock is the same as the preceding title, and it is the act of borrowing supplies from stockbrokers to meet your requirements, intending to sell them to other interested purchasers. Shorting a shop does not happen all of the time; it usually occurs when the business is overvalued.

The danger of this trade is that a broker or a buyer might lose a lot of money. Shorting your stock is a high-risk, time-consuming approach; if it succeeds, you'll have all of your profits and nothing to lose. If it doesn't work out, you'll be sorry and wish you hadn't taken that choice in the first place.

Before making a stock transaction, double-checking stock market rumors is also a good idea. The fact is that holding your investment for a long time is safer.

CONCLUSION

Trading options, to put it simply, is neither a kind of gambling nor is it considered to be "high finance." If you approach trading in the right way, you should be able to earn money practically every year of your trading career, regardless of whether the market is up or down. There aren't many trading techniques that can make such a claim. The ability to comprehend and manage risk, on the other hand, is critical to achieving success. Every time you enter into a transaction, you transfer risk to the other party. Selling options entails taking on the risk of the person who purchased the options. Because this is the side of the deal that most commonly gives money-making chances, it is your responsibility as a trader to determine if the price you are getting paid for an option is sufficient compensation for the risk you are taking.

We aim, with the authoring of this book, to have provided a high-level overview of the key mechanics of options trading.

Regardless of the kind of investment you choose, constantly do thorough research. It is necessary to do research. What you need will boost your chances of making the best investment selection possible. After all, "knowledge is power," as the adage goes. The more your understanding of something, the more probable it is that you will forecast its movement in the market. It is for this reason that research is necessary. It will enable you to choose if something is worth your time and money or not. Recall that you are working with a constantly changing market, and it is only proper that you keep yourself informed of the most recent advancements and changes in the industry. Research is the most effective method of doing this.

With the potential for bigger rewards, trading options may help you diversify your portfolio while increasing your returns.

Thank you for making it to the end of this book. Try to gain confidence in this manner before moving on to an online trade simulator. You will trade here in the same way that you would on a broker's platform. You will, however, use virtual money. Only after you have thoroughly understood how to trade options should you attempt to go live and trade on a live platform. The best approach is to choose your favorite strategy and then work on improving it.

Trading success cannot be achieved in a short time. Before applying your knowledge in trading procedures, you must carefully follow the instructions and suggestions. If you follow the instructions in this book, you will quickly start making good profits. Trading can be extremely profitable if done correctly.

Good luck.

Scan these **QR CODEs** with your smartphone and download your GIFTS (digital version/pdf):

NFT for

BEGINNERS

(digital version)

OPTIONS TRADING

7 BOOKS in 1

(digital version)